THE TEACHING
OF ENGLISH
ABROAD

By F. G. FRENCH, C.B.E.

Part I: Aims and Methods

Oxford University Press

Oxford University Press, Ely House, London W. 1

GLASGOW NEW YORK TORONTO MELBOURNE WELLINGTON
CAPE TOWN DELHI IBADAN NAIROBI DAR ES SALAAM LUSAKA ADDIS ABABA
BOMBAY CALCUTTA MADRAS KARACHI LAHORE DACCA
KUALA LUMPUR SINGAPORE HONG KONG TOKYO

First published 1948
Thirteenth impression 1975

Printed in Great Britain by Richard Clay (The Chaucer Press), Ltd.,
Bungay, Suffolk

CONTENTS

INTRODUCTION

This small book is one of a set of three, all addressed to the teacher in his classroom, offering him a variety of practical teaching devices.

The first book discusses the main principles of language teaching and their application to modern practice. It uses the experience which has been gathered over many years by teachers in Africa, India, Burma, Malaya, Japan and China, as well as that of teachers in America. In order to keep the book short and simple there is no discussion of the different ' methods ' which have been tried in different places at various times ; those principles which are now accepted by successful teachers are explained, and suggestions are made for using them in the classroom.

The methods of teaching the other school subjects (arithmetic, geography, and the rest) give rise to much less argument than the teaching of English, for two reasons. In the first place, the matter to be taught is fixed and arranges itself in a natural order for teaching. Arithmetic begins with number and goes on to the four rules—there is no other way of teaching arithmetic. But English is not like that. In the second place, teachers of English have strong likes and dislikes which come from their own experience and from the way in which their teachers taught them when they were

1

beginners. Some find difficulty in giving lessons without a reading-book open in front of every pupil ; some would give much time to easy poems and rhymes ; some would pay most attention to reading or to writing. It will be found that the arguments put forward by these very good teachers are often not quite fair ; they push into the background anything which does not support that side of the work which they like best.

This book does not try to argue ; it simply sets out those kinds of work which many thousands of teachers have found to be successful. Do these things first ; you can add to them all the other things which you particularly like.

The first problem is, ' What must we put in and what can we safely leave out of our English lessons ? ' In this book the matter to be put into the lessons has been selected as follows :—

(a) those sentence-patterns which occur most frequently in straightforward English speech and print. The difficult sentence-patterns (which are not really necessary, because the same thing can be said in simpler patterns) have been left out.

(b) those words which pass the test of the highest measure of usefulness in general English, with some more words connected with the pupils' own life and surroundings. Words which are not included in the ' Report on Vocabulary Selection, 1936 ' have been left out. The words remaining are plentiful, for all purposes.

(c) those grammatical points which are essential when judged by the test that English depends upon word-order and upon ' structural words ' (pronouns, prepositions, auxiliary verbs) to form its sentence-patterns, and uses only a very few inflexions (for number, for degree, and in verbs). Other grammatical topics are left out.

The second problem is, ' What principles must we follow in choosing the things we shall do in the classroom ? ' In this book, these principles have been taken :—

(*a*) the importance of forming language habits, particularly the habit of arranging words in English standard sentence-patterns, to replace the sentence-patterns of the pupils' own language.

(*b*) the importance of speech as the necessary means of fixing firmly all groundwork.

(*c*) the importance of the pupils' activity rather than the activity of the teacher.

The third problem is, ' What classroom practices will best turn these principles into actual lesson-work ? ' In this book, those classroom practices are described which have been proved successful in the hands of ordinary teachers. It is understood that this book will be read by only a few British teachers and American teachers; it is written for those teachers who have not the advantage of using English as their mother-tongue, but have had to learn it themselves as a foreign language. Such teachers find it very difficult to do in class what an American or British teacher finds it very easy to do. Therefore the classroom practices here described are those which are used successfully by teachers to whom English is a foreign language.

Finally, because the book is short, it can only offer help ; it cannot contain everything that can be done in lesson time. The reader should therefore think over each Chapter and add to it anything that he can pick up from his friends and from other teachers and other schools. If he knows clearly what he is aiming at, and how far he can hope to get in his teaching of English, he will be able to add many useful things to the groundwork which is here offered to him.

The second book deals in detail with the difficulties of teachers responsible for the first three years of English.

The third book does the same for those with classes of senior pupils in the last three years of a six (or seven) years' course.

These last two books are related in particular to the Oxford English Courses for Africa and Malaya.

CHAPTER I

THE TEACHER'S AIM

1. English is rapidly becoming a world language. It is the mother-tongue of more than 200,000,000 people, and in addition it is spoken and read by many millions of Europeans, Africans, Chinese, Indians, Japanese, and South Americans as a second language. The flow of new pupils never stops ; not counting British and American children, about 20,000;000 boys and girls begin learning English every year.

Everything of importance which happens day by day is printed in English in newspapers, or spoken in English over the radio, all over the world ; and this is true in the great European countries as well as in countries in the East and in the West. A person who can speak English will find somebody who can understand him wherever he may go ; anyone who can read English can keep in touch with all the world without leaving his own home.

2. It is clearly the teacher's duty to do everything possible to give his pupils, even though the time may be short, a command of English which will be sufficient and lasting. The teacher cannot hope to make every pupil speak, read and write like an American or a British person ; the aim must be limited in order that it may be reached. There are four clear aims which are within the limits of possibility ; speaking, understanding what is spoken, reading, and writing.

(1) We try to give the pupil the ability to speak English within a limited vocabulary, and correctly within the most useful sentence-patterns. Speech is essential because language is a spoken

5

thing. For every word that is written or read, millions of words are spoken ; writing and printing are only speech reduced to black signs.

(2) We try to give the pupil the ability to understand what is spoken. This is a wider task than the first, for it brings in a wider vocabulary—all those extra words which are known, but which are not remembered for immediate use. It also has an obvious practical value. A learner who says ' Please speak more slowly ' has not been taught to listen.

(3) We try to give the pupil the ability to read. This means a great increase in the number of words which are known when seen but which are not ready for immediate use in speech. Reading includes everything that is included in speech, and much more besides.

(4) We try to give the pupil the ability to write ; this is the hardest task of all, and for many learners the least important. To speech, listening, and reading, it adds spelling, handwriting, and punctuation.

3. Speech is the groundwork ; all the rest are built up from it. Through speech, the pupil learns to make the direct connection between the English word or phrase and the object, action, or idea it bears. He learns the habit of using words in the correct sentence-patterns and phrase-patterns ; and he can learn this in no other way. The ' common errors ' which are so plentiful in pupils' work are due to the fact that the teacher has relied too much on reading and the reading-book where words are seen singly, and not enough on speech where there are no single words, but only phrase-patterns and sentence-patterns.

We cannot see or learn the pattern of a sentence clearly if we look at the words one at a time ; but in speech we hear (and learn) this :—

welookat thewords oneatatime

and that *is* the pattern of that sentence.

4. Listening is a part of speaking and is just as important. In listening, the sentence-patterns of English are to be found in the way the words run together. They are often made very clear by the stress which the speaker puts on important words :

One of the *boys* did it.

or in the way in which the speaker's voice goes up and down : for example, in the question-pattern

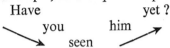

We learn our own language by listening ; it is the only method a baby uses in the first stages.

5. Reading is a difficult skill to learn because once again the sentence-pattern is the important thing, but it is hidden by the printing of the separate words. A good reader does not look at each word separately, but he gathers at one look each part of the sentence-pattern :

He gathers at one look each part of the sentence-pattern.

But the little child is compelled at first to look at almost every letter to be sure of its shape. It is the teacher's aim to make this stage as short as possible.

6. Writing is the last skill the child requires, and in our teaching it therefore follows the other skills.

Points to think about and discuss

1. What is the meaning of the phrase ' a second language ' ? Why is it useful to have a second

language in your country—what practical value is there in it ? Why do people in large countries like Russia and China learn English as their second language ?

2. If you had to teach your own language to an American, how would you begin ? Would you begin by reading ?

3. When they leave school, pupils take up different kinds of work. Make a list of the different kinds of employment which will probably be taken up by the pupils of a school well-known to you. Consider in what ways a knowledge of English will be useful to each of them.

4. How would you advise a pupil leaving school to use (a) the radio, (b) the cinema, to improve his English ?

What radio programmes can you hear yourself, and where ? Do you make the greatest possible use of those opportunities ?

Consider how to form a Radio Club among your friends.

For the practical teacher

1. Within reach of every school there are sure to be European or American missionaries, merchants, officials or business-men. These receive regularly a supply of newspapers, magazines, and catalogues from their homelands. They will be ready and pleased to give such papers to your school when they have finished with them.

One or two pupils in the class may be appointed ' British Correspondent ' or ' American Correspondent ' or ' Indian Correspondent ' with the duty of calling upon these friends of the school and collecting papers, magazines and pictures from the part of the world for which they are responsible.

2. All schools, all over the world, are pleased to receive material from other countries. Through the foreign friends who supply you with British or American magazines, try to get into touch with schools in those countries and exchange newspapers, trade catalogues, and other English material.

3. The same methods may be used to obtain small photographs and picture-postcards, which should be pinned up on the classroom wall.

CHAPTER II

THE BONES OF ENGLISH

1.   A dictionary is not a language ; and a foreign language is not just a great heap of thousands of strange words.   Many words are common to all languages ;   for example, the word *telephone* can be understood in at least two hundred languages without any change in its pronunciation.   Languages certainly consist of words, but they employ those words in sentences in very different ways.   A practical example may be considered :—

There are many kinds of lamps ;   some are lit by electricity, some burn paraffin, some burn petrol, and some use heavy oil.

Similarly, there are many kinds of oil.   Some kinds of oil are used as food and are mixed with other kinds of food in cooking ;   another kind of oil is used for keeping engines clean ;   another kind is used, like petrol, to work engines ; another kind is used in lamps.

After that explanation, consider carefully how you say in your own language these two sentences, having in mind the particular kind of lamp and the particular kind of oil :—

(*a*)   Please give me an oil lamp.

(*b*)   Please give me some lamp oil.

Examine the expression in your own language. Now examine it in English and notice that the whole meaning of what the speaker asks for is changed merely by changing the order of the words in English :

oil lamp,   lamp oil.

2.   That little exercise shows that the English teacher must study very carefully the ways in which English words are used ;   and that to learn the meaning

10

of the word is not sufficient. The exercise shows also that the English teacher must also think continually of the ways in which his own language uses words in sentences, so that he may help his pupils when the English way and the vernacular way are different.

3. For this purpose it is necessary to ask, ' What ways are used in English to fit words together into sentences ? '

The answer is in three parts, and the first part is shown by the example just given.

In English *the order of the words* is very important.

1. Kazi saw Daud. Daud saw Kazi.
2. Fish eat. Eat fish !

3. a foot long

   a long foot

The first principle used in English for fitting words into sentences is *word-order*.

4. In many languages both the spelling and the pronunciation of a verb are changed to show whether one person or more than one person is meant. How do you say in your own language :—

I go, You go, Two of us go, They go ?

Notice that in English the verb *go* does not change here.

How do you ask in your own language :—

Did he go ? Will he go ? Does he go ?

Notice that in English the verb *go* does not change here; but a different small word is used to show the change in meaning :— *did, will, does.*

How do you say in your own language :—

at the house, to the house, in the house, from the house ?

Notice again that in English the chief word *house* is not changed ; but a small word is used two spaces

11

away from it :—*at, to, in, from.* (at the house ; at my house ; at the other house.)

This gives the second part of the answer to the question, ' What ways are used in English to fit words together into sentences ? ' The second part of the answer is that, in English, words do not *usually* change when they are put into sentences ; instead of changing the spelling and the pronunciation, English uses small helping words like *do, will, to, at, from.* These words are called structural words because they are necessary to the structure of the English sentence.

The second principle in English is *the use of structural words.*

5. However, there are a few changes in words, which have to be learned :—

    (1) in verbs : I go, You go,

                    She *goes*, He *goes*, It *goes.*

        I answer now. I answer*ed* yesterday.

     but there is no change in :

        I went, You went, She went, He went, It went

    (2) in nouns : One boy, two boy*s*, a boy'*s* book.

    (3) in adjectives and adverbs : quick, quick*er,* quick*est.*

This gives us the third part of the answer. English also uses a few word changes to show various meanings, when words are fitted into sentences.

The third principle in English is *the use of a small number of inflexions.*

6. The bones of the English language are therefore of three kinds :—

    (*a*) Word-order.   (*b*) Structural words.

    (*c*) A few inflexions.

7. Of these three, by far the most important is word-order, because word-order in English is fixed,

and upon it depends the plan of each standard model sentence.

This gives a very important principle for the guidance of the English teacher. Because word-order in English is fixed, and because word-order is the most important thing in every English sentence, therefore the models for the different kinds of English sentences are fixed also. And these can be taught to the pupils as soon as they begin to learn the language.

As examples, study the plan of each of these model sentences :—

Mr. Kazi is	working
	angry
	a teacher
	in this classroom

There is one model :

| A | B | C |
| Mr. Kazi | is | ... |

for those different kinds of sentence ; and having learned the model, the pupil is able to make up at once many hundreds of sentences.

That lion / was not / sleeping.
My teacher / will be / very pleased with me.
My father / became / headman of the village.
Your sister / has not been / in this town.

8. After word-order and sentence-patterns, the next important thing in English is structural words.
These are :

(*a*) the pronouns : I, me, he, her, their, some, any (and many others)

(*b*) the prepositions : in, on, under, at, from (and many others)

(*c*) the helping verbs : do, have, be, will, can, may (and many others) (*d*) structural adjectives and adverbs :

> a, the, this, that, all, each (and many others)
>
> ago, again, also, even, ever, no, not (and many others)

These structural words are used more frequently in English than any other words. In 100 ordinary sentences there may be as many as 300 prepositions, 200 pronouns, and 100 other structural words—a total of 600 structural words in 100 sentences.

This fact gives another valuable guide to the English teacher : structural words must be taught as early as possible and must be constantly practised, because of their great frequency and high importance.

9. Word changes in English are few in number. They must be taught in the order of their importance : changes for the plural ; changes in verbs ; changes for comparison.

10. To summarize this chapter : the English language employs three important methods of using words in sentences. Because one of these ways is the use of word-order, sentence-patterns are fixed in English, and these fixed patterns can be taught even to very young pupils.

Inflexions in English are few in number, and these can be introduced into the lessons in the order of their usefulness.

Points to think about and discuss

1. Show in sentences the difference between :
(*a*) I and me ; (*b*) He and him ; (*c*) She and her ;
(*d*) They and them.

Notice the importance of word-order in your sentences.

2. Language is a spoken thing, not something written or printed by means of letters. Some teachers tell their pupils that the plural in English is generally formed by adding the letter *s*. Prove that this is not the whole truth, by considering the *sounds* in these :—

    (*a*) cat, cats ;   book, books ;   map, maps

    (*b*) boy, boys ;   hour, hours ;   key, keys

    (*c*) nose, noses ; horse, horses ;   piece, pieces

3. Look up these structural words in a good dictionary and count the number of different meanings given to each :—

    to, for, at ;   make, get, go, may

4. Here are the 24 most useful and most frequently used words in the English language :—

a	be	is	that	will	and
are	but	it	the	with	you
as	for	not	this	have	your
at	in	of	to	on	me

Notice that they are all structural words. There are no nouns among them.

Use each one in a sentence and try to make sentences which show different meanings. A good dictionary will help you.

For example, for the word *a* :—

    A fish may cost *a* shilling *a* pound.

5. (*a*) When an adjective is added to a noun, what is the general rule regarding word-order ?

(*b*) What is the rule when an adverb is added to a verb ?

Do these three adverbs *always* follow the general rule :—

> always   never   often

6. Are there pronouns in your own language similar to I, me, he, him, etc. ? If so, what are they, and how are they used ?

How would you teach a young English pupil to translate into your language : (*a*) I ; (*b*) me ; (*c*) she ; (*d*) he ?

7. Give reasons why the first inflexion to be taught in English should be the inflexion for Number : boy, boys ; pen, pens. Give your reasons under these heads :—

    i.   Value for revision ; ii. Use of objects ;

    iii.   Opportunities for action by the pupils ;

    iv.   Training in listening.

8. How are plurals expressed in your language ? Compare with the English method. How would you teach an Englishman the plural forms in your language?

9. Make a list of words which are the same in your language and in English, like *telephone*. In your language do these words obey the English rules for forming the plural, or do they obey the rules of your own language ?

10. Do adjectives change in your language ? How do you say (looking at the word *good*) :—

    a good boy ; a good girl ; good boys ; good girls ;
    a good answer ; a good train ;
    He is a good man. Kazi bought a good horse.
    Daud went to the good man's funeral.
    The teacher gave prizes to several good pupils.

For the practical teacher

1. The importance of word-order can be kept before the class by placing on the classroom walls strips of brown paper each illustrating a sentence-pattern :—

Model No. 3		
Mr. Kazi	is	working
This	is	a book

The pupils suggest additions to each column, as they meet them in their work. The strips should remain on the walls for only one week and then be removed. They may be put back again a month later. The pupils pay no attention to strips which are kept on the walls for too long.

2. For sentence-patterns, an interesting model can be made by movable strips through slots. The pupils can make these for themselves, but the teacher must see that the words are correct.

One strip can be moved at a time, or two strips, or three.

3. Prepositions can be drilled (always in phrase-patterns or sentence-patterns) in many ways. For example, a square is drawn on the blackboard. The teacher makes a dot, or an arrow in various positions, and the class gives the correct phrase-pattern :—

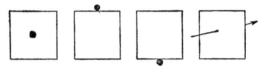

in the square ; through the square, etc.

4. A fly may be made to travel in a picture, and the class gives the correct phrase-pattern for each position :—

> through the window ; towards the door ;
> up the door ; round the lamp ; between the legs
> of the table ; etc.

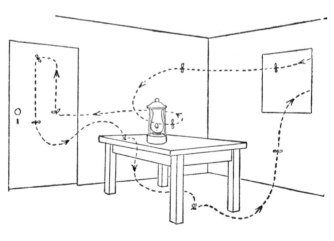

CHAPTER III

WORDS : I. LEARNING WORDS

1. It may seem that the learning of a new English word is a very simple business : English word— vernacular meaning ; but that is by no means the case. There are no less than eight different things which become linked together in the mind in the act of learning just one new word. These eight sides to the learning process are :—

(1) the object itself, or a picture of it ;

(2) the nearest translation in the pupil's own language ;

(3) the sound of the English name of the object ;

(4) the act of watching the teacher's lips and mouth when he speaks the word ;

(5) the act of moving the muscles of the tongue, lips, and throat, when the pupil says the word himself ;

(6) the act of watching the teacher's hand as he writes the word. This is very important indeed if the written letters of the pupil's language are not the same as the written letters of English.

(7) the study of the written or printed appearance of the word when the pupil first sees it ;

(8) the act of controlling the muscles of the hand and wrist in writing the word, when the pupil first writes it.

2. The human mind is able to remember a thing because it makes associations or links between the new thing which is being learned and things already

known. For example, *knife* is remembered because in the mind it is joined up with the old ideas of cutting, of sharpness, of brightness, of wood (for the handle), of steel (for the blade), and with all other ideas about things used for cutting, and perhaps with one particular real knife ; and in addition the hearing, speaking and writing of the word *knife*.

Thus, in the process of learning a new word, the mind links together the eight items described in paragraph 1 above, and we remember best those things concerning which our minds have made the strongest links.

It is clear that if his teaching is to be successful, the teacher must know what is going on in the pupil's mind, and he must do those things which will help the pupil's mind to join together all the eight sides of the act of learning.

3. To make it easier to understand, the formation of the network of links may be split up into five parts :

First, there is a set of three links which join the object (or picture) with the sound of the word and with the appearance of the written word (Nos. 1, 3, and 7 in paragraph 1) :—

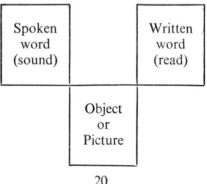

Second, there is a set of three links which join the English spoken word and the English written word with the vernacular nearest translation :—

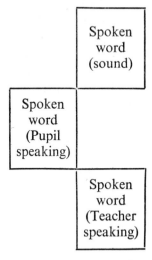

Third, when the pupil speaks the word himself, there is a set of three links which join the sound of the spoken word (heard in the mind) with the muscular act of saying it and with the sight of the teacher's lips and mouth saying it :—

Fourth, when the pupil learns to write the word, there is a set of three links which join the shape of the written word (when looked at) with the sight of the teacher's hand writing it (especially if this is different in some way from the writing of the vernacular) and with the muscular act of the pupil writing it himself:

Written word (read)	
	Written word (by the Teacher)
Written word (by the Pupil)	

Fifth, there is a set of five links which join all these with the object or picture :—

Spoken word (sound)		Written word (read)
	Object or Picture	
Spoken word (by the Pupil)		Written word (by the Pupil)

4. All these links (except those connected with the written words) are built up in a pupil's mind even when he is learning his own language during his babyhood. But he does it all by himself, for he has no teacher. His mother very rarely takes up an object and teaches the child to say its name. The child learns by his own efforts.

It is important to notice also that he does not learn by hearing one word spoken by itself; he hears sentences and long conversations (which at first he does not understand) but he very rarely hears one word spoken alone.

Keeping these points in mind, the process by which a baby learns the words of his own language may be studied in detail, in order to see how it works, and so find guidance for our own teaching.

5. The first step is *listening*. The child sees grown-up people looking at, pointing to, and touching an object while talking rapidly. He sees that the object in which the grown-ups are interested is (say) a and he hears one sound coming several times in the middle of all the noises the grown-ups are making. He connects that sound with the object. This happens many times, and with various objects, but the child remains silent.

He watches his mother, and the others, making the sound ' SPOON', and after a time he may be observed attempting to copy them, but not, as yet, with any purpose in view.

The second step is speaking, and it comes when the child desires to play with the object and wishes to call the attention of his mother. He then attempts to say the word out loud, for the first time, and with a purpose in view. He finds he is successful, and this pleases him. He repeats the word many times, just for the joy of it. It becomes almost a game, but *always* with the object within touching distance, or at least within sight.

The final stage in this part of the process is reached when the child is able to think of the object, and to call for it, even when it is not in sight.

· 6. The same kind of thing occurs with the names of actions ; and the first verbs learned are certainly the names of actions which the child wishes to perform himself : *walk, go, drink, eat,* and (at an early stage) *want.*

All these are first heard mixed up in the conversations of grown-ups ; and though the talk is not understood, the actions are observed, and they are performed by the child himself. In that way, the direct link between the sound and the idea is made, together with the other links of watching his mother's lips saying the word and the feel of his own throat muscles trying to say it too.

And always there is a great deal of repetition and practice.

7. Using this as a guide to classroom work in teaching a foreign language, we may notice five important principles :—

(1) *Listening :* hearing the sound and watching the lips of the speaker ;

(2) *Trial and Practice :* the word becomes fixed by the child's own use of it, many times. He cannot get possession of it merely by hearing it or seeing it ;

(3) The word is always heard with *the object or the action in sight,* and it is always heard in a sentence ;

24

(4) *The sentences themselves are very important* to the child.   For example : ' I want . . .' In this way he gets possession of his first sentence-patterns :—

I want   a drink.   I want   to walk. And the method by which he learns the sentence-pattern is exactly the same as that by which he learns the names of objects.

(5) In learning his own language, the child, for several years does not read and does not write.   *He begins to read and to write after he has learned the words and the sentence-patterns and phrase-patterns.*

8.   The study of the way in which the mind builds round a new word a number of links which join it up with old words so that it can be remembered, and the study of the way in which a little child learns his own language, both give the same guidance for the method to be followed in the early stages of teaching a foreign language (but, of course, in the classroom, the whole process can be covered much more rapidly) :—

(1) *a.* Listening before speaking ;
    b. Not ears alone, but ears and eyes.   Listening must be going on whilst the pupils see the object or the action, or at least a picture of it ;
    c. Listening must be *listening to sentences.* even if these are not understood at first. The word must be learned in a sentence-pattern or a phrase-pattern.

(2) After listening, speaking.   Tongue, ears, and eyes are now all employed.   If the new word is connected with an action, the child must

25

perform it, or see it performed, at the same time as he speaks.

(3) There is no hurry for the Reading Book. Words and sentence-patterns are fixed first by listening and speaking ; reading and writing come afterwards.

Reading is only a means of fixing still more firmly what has already been fixed by listening and speech. New material must not be given to the child for the first time in printed form, but always in spoken form.

Points to think about and discuss

1. Consider the importance of pictures in the English classroom :—

(*a*) First there are the wall-charts which contain large-size copies of some of the pictures printed in the pupils' own books. Why are such large-size copies necessary ? How can they be used ?

(*b*) Second there are the pictures in the Reader, especially where these are chosen to illustrate particular words. The pictures are chosen (i) to help with reading, (ii) to help with pronunciation—notice the vowel sounds in lamp, laughing, lion, load, lorry (letter *l* pictures).

(*c*) Which is better, a picture or the object itself ? The answer to that question is not easy ; consider the word *hat*. How would you meet this difficulty in your own classroom ?

2. Do you think that two little children, living in the same town but in different houses, will learn the same words in their own language in the first three years of life ? Give reasons, and examples.

3. What rules would you suggest in your own

classroom for the proper storage and care of your collection of pictures ?

4. Examine your series of Class Readers, Books I and II, and find out what sentence-patterns are taught in them.

5. Why is it important that the child should hear other voices speaking English besides his teacher's voice and his own ? How can this be done in your classroom ?

6. Make a list of the first twenty words which a little child in your country will learn in his own language ; then make a list of the first twenty words which he will learn when he begins English. Are the words in the two lists the same ? If not, why not ? Why are those the first twenty *English* words he learns ?

7. Prepare a list of the first twenty nouns and the first twenty verbs you think a child should learn when beginning English. Give reasons for your lists.

8. You are going to a new school where you will be responsible for teaching English in the first year :

(*a*) Make a list of the objects which you will collect and use in teaching words and phrases ;

(*b*) Make a list of the pictures you will need.
Compare your lists with those made by your friends.

9. Look at the lists you made for Exercise 8 and decide which of the objects and pictures (more than one in each case) you would use in these lessons :—

   i. a lesson on the verb *hold up* ;

   ii. a lesson on the verbs *open* and *shut* ;

   iii. a lesson on the words *in, on, under*.

10. Do you think the methods described in this Chapter III should be applied also in classes of grown-up men and women who wish to learn English and have to begin at the beginning ? Will the words

taught in the first ten lessons be exactly the same for them ? If not, why not ?

For the practical teacher

1. In some Readers (for example the Oxford series), there are pages of pictures called '*The Picture Dictionary*'. Use it in these ways :—

(*a*) for pronunciation :
Point out the vowel sounds with which each picture is connected :—

eating   egg   (ee   ĕ)
fish   fly   frog   (ĭ   ī   ŏ)

Point out the pictures (or make the children find them) which, beginning with a different letter, illustrate a given sound :—

(vowel ī)   knife   writing   lion
(sound f)   knife   face   laugh

(*b*) for sentence-patterns :
The children practise a given sentence-pattern, using the pictures. It is very important to teach the rapid speech-pattern as well as the fully printed pattern :—

What / is / this ?   This / is / a (lion).
What's this ?   Thisisa lion.
He / is / laughing.   What / is / he / doing ?
He's laughing.   What's he doing ?

2. Pupils with baby brothers and sisters will be pleased to be allowed to report new words those babies are learning in their own language. The equivalent sentence-patterns can then be learned by the class in English.

3. Teachers wishing to study the procedure to be followed in Listening lessons are referred to my book '*First Year English* ; *What and How to Teach* ' (Oxford University Press).

CHAPTER IV

WORDS : II.   THE VOCABULARY

1.   It is obvious that the number of words which can be learned in a given time is limited ; and from the many tens of thousands of English words some must be chosen for teaching and a huge number must be rejected. Either of two methods may be employed by a text-book writer in making this selection :—

   i. He may choose a vocabulary ' island '. Class-books written in this way use a limited vocabulary which, like an island, is complete in itself. The difficulty, of course, is to get into the ' island ' all the words which people wish to see there.

   ii. He may choose a ' foundation ' vocabulary. Class books written in this way use a limited vocabulary which will enable the teacher to teach all the necessary sentence-patterns and phrase-patterns, and will therefore provide the pupil with a sound groundwork to which he can add new words as often as he likes ; and he can go on doing so after he has left school.

This book follows the second method.

2.   A very great deal of work has been done, all over the world, on this problem of selecting the words which should be taught to beginners ; and as a result a list (called '*An Interim Report on Vocabulary Selection*, 1936 ') has been made of 2,000 words chosen for these reasons :—

   (1) They are the words most frequently used by people whose mother-tongue is English.
   (2) They include all the structural words.
   (3) They are words which are useful in any country

and any climate.

(4) They include words most useful in explaining the meanings of other, less frequently used, words.

(5) They include words which are useful because other words can be built from them. For example :—

   spot, spotted, spotless, spotty, unspotted.

3. These 2,000 words cannot all be taught in the first year ; it is therefore necessary to decide which should be taught first, in the first year, and which words should be taught in the second year, and so on. Obviously, the most useful words should be taught first.

Unfortunately, the 100 words which are the most useful and most frequently necessary for the construction of sentences, are the most difficult to teach. The list of the 100 most useful words contains 95 structural words, no ordinary verbs like *walk* or *speak*, and only 5 nouns :— *day*, *time*, *man*, *year*, *way*.

It is impossible to teach these very important structural words (like *a*, *are*, *have*, *in*, *is*, *of*, *this*, *you*, *any*, *do*, *my*, *there*, *come*, *get*, *here*, *no*, *other*, *what*), without using some ordinary nouns and ordinary verbs to fill up the places in the sentence-patterns and phrase-patterns.

In view of what was explained in Chapter III about the ways in which new words are learned and remembered, the ordinary nouns and verbs required to make up sentence-patterns must be connected with the learner's own surroundings and interests, even if these words (such as *inkpot*, *blackboard*, *point to*) are not very high up on the list of words most frequently used in ordinary conversation.

30

4. It is now possible to select the words which are to be taught in the English lessons, beginning with the first year. They must be :—

(a) words with a very high measure of usefulness in making sentences ;

(b) additional words connected with the pupils' own surroundings and interests (including words useful in story-telling).

The words in a good series of class-readers are selected in this way.

5. A straightforward list of the words to be taught is very useful, and every teacher should keep a notebook in which he enters, after each lesson, the new words which have been given to the pupils. The words should be listed in two ways :— first, lesson by lesson ; and secondly, in alphabetical order.

But it is not sufficient merely to write the new word alone in such a list, for one word may have many different uses, and each use should be entered separately.

Consider the sentence : I was looking at the wrong *line*. That sentence takes on a different meaning according to whether the speaker was looking at (a) a book or (b) a drawing, or (c) a regiment of soldiers, or (d) a poem, or (e) a railway. No word has a full meaning when it stands alone ; it gets most of its meaning from the words around it.

For this reason a bare list of words is not of much use ; and a word-list should always contain illustrations and examples.

For example :—

All : all the books   all at once
      all of it   all together
      tell me all about it all alone
      all right   it is all gone (=finished).

Similarly, it is a useful practice to bring together the words belonging to one head-word. For example :

Bed : bedclothes
      bedding
      bedroom
      bedtime.

6. The words (other than structural words) which have to be learned fall into three main classes : (*a*) words for things ; (*b*) words for actions ; and (*c*) words for qualities.

The teacher should note, for his own information, that each of these classes contains three or four different kinds of words.

(*a*) Words for things include :
   i. simple nouns : table, chair, sky
   ii. compound nouns : workmen, sunset, football
   iii. words formed from Class (*b*) : teacher, growth, punishment
   iv. words formed from Class (*c*) : goodness, truth, depth

(*b*) Words for actions include :
   i. simple verbs : walk, sing, write
   ii. verbs formed with structural words : look for, look at, pick up, listen to
   iii. words formed from Class (*a*) : enjoy, paint, brush
   iv. words formed from Class (*c*) : weaken, soften

(*c*) Words for qualities include :
   i. simple adjectives and adverbs : tall, short, quick

ii. words formed from Class (*a*) : dirty, rainy, friendly

iii. words formed from Class (*b*) : broken, torn, tired, sleeping (*child*)

7. The advantage of making these various lists is that each of them provides the mind with one more ' link ' or ' association ' and in that way the memory for the word is strengthened.

It is for this reason that the pupils should be encouraged to make their own lists of various kinds, the same word appearing in two or three lists. The following are suggested as examples of the many various ways in which words may be grouped :—

Names of occupations		*Words connected with the railway*	
teacher	doctor	engine	carriage
farmer	sailor	rail	ticket
	etc.	guard	etc.

Parents, Babies and Homes				*Places of work*	
father	mother	child	home	doctor ...	hospital
lion	lioness	cub	den	teacher ...	school
cock	hen	chicken	nest	clerk.	office
	etc.			sailor	ship
				etc.	

Word families

joy : enjoy, joyful, enjoyment, enjoying

work : workman, workshop, workless, working

etc.

Containers		*Opposites*	
bottle, basket,		long	short
box, tin, cupboard		wide	narrow
etc.		etc.	

Pupils in the third year will take a great interest in making such lists, and there will be considerable competition to determine who can make the best lists.

8. To sum up this chapter : Words to be taught in the first years of English must be carefully chosen on the grounds of greatest usefulness. This choice is made for the teacher by the writer of the classbook, if he knows his business. Pupils should be helped to remember new words, not only by all the various methods (listening, speaking, action, dictation) used in the classroom, but also by providing a large number of ' links ' in the child's mind between the new word and old words already known. And all the time the new word must be presented *always* in a sentence-pattern or a phrase-pattern.

Points to think about and discuss

1. It has been found that, on the average, there are three prepositions in every sentence ; that is to say, you require about 300 prepositions to make 100 sentences.

The prepositions which occur most frequently are these nine :

of, in, with, at, by, to, for, on, from

Each of these is used in a very large number of different ways. The best (and largest) English dictionary gives :

of, 63 different meanings ; *in*, 40 ; *with*, 40 ; *at*, 39 ; *by*, 39 ; *to*, 33 ; *for*, 31 ; *on*, 29 ; *from*, 15.

This proves that it is far more useful to spend time in learning how to use these important little structural words than to pile up large numbers of nouns ; in fact, it is often impossible to use a noun without adding a preposition to it.

These structural words are useful because they make phrase-patterns :—

Add further examples to each of these patterns :

    i.   a *bottle of* ink ;
   ii.   I am *afraid of* him ;
  iii.   it was *kind of* him to go ;
  iv.   *made of* brass ;
   v.   a *class of* boys ;
  vi.   the *leg of* a dog ;
 vii.   a *part of* it ;
viii.   the *edge of* it.

2. Special care must be given to structural verbs. It is dangerous to think that when your pupils have learned to read one of these, they need not be taught any more about it. Consider the meanings of these sentences, and the changes in the meaning of the structural word *had* :—

> The boy had two books.
> The boy had finished his work.
> The boy had to buy a new book.
> The boy had his leg cut off.
> The boy had to have his leg cut off.
> The boy had had his work corrected by the teacher.

Consider in the same way :—

> get a book ; get cold ; get hold of ; get a sum right ; get him to do it ; get something mended ; get your hair cut ; get better ; get away ; get on ; get up (*rise from bed*) ; have got to do it.

Each of these different meanings really makes a new phrase-pattern ; so that the way to meet the difficulties of structural verbs is to drill the pupils in the phrase-patterns in which they occur.

3. Use your dictionary to make similar lists of meanings for :—

work	use	up	turn	time	take	stop
so	set	put	over	out	on	off
make	leave	keep	in	have	go	by
fill	drive	to	cut	come	back	as

4. Consider and write down examples of the different kinds of lists of words a teacher should have in his own notebook (*see paragraphs* 6 *and* 7 *above*).

For the practical teacher

1. The movable strip may be used for word-building. Words are added to the strip as the pupils meet them in their work :

2. A test which pupils very much enjoy is 'Find the wrong word.' Like this :—

In the following lists one word is wrong because it does not belong to the same class as the other words. Find the wrong word :—

  i. dog, cow, hen, elephant
    (*Answer* : hen : It is the only word which names a bird.)

36

ii. eye, nose, mouth, hand

> (*Answer* : hand : All the other words name parts of the face.)

3. In English, it is very easy to use a noun as a verb.

> This is red *paint* (noun).   *Paint* a picture (verb).

The pupils may sometimes be asked to find out how many words they have collected in their lists which can be used both as nouns and as verbs.

4. Tables can be used for practising structural words in their right places in a sentence-pattern. The pupils can suggest other words to add to the lists :—

This is	a my his Kazi's Lily's etc.	book	I am not	strong big clever etc.	enough to do it
Put it	on off back etc.		I want	to do it to go there to learn English etc.	

CHAPTER V

THE FORMATION OF SENTENCES

1. A sentence is a group of words which are fitted together—

so as to
- make a statement : I like this.
- ask a question : Have you finished your work ?
- make a request : Please take this.

Each word in a sentence has its own meaning, but it takes on additional meanings from the words around it. The word *like* has a meaning but there is a difference between *I like this* and *I like you ;* the difference is caused by the neighbouring words. In fact, meaning is given not by single words standing alone, but by groups of words stuck together in lumps :—

Themaninthecar   hadtofireashot   tosavehislife.

It has been shown in Chapter III that words (whether in your own or in a foreign language) are best learned in sentences, or at least in phrases.

2. Every language has its own ways of fitting words together to form sentences, and these ways take shape as sentence-patterns. The word *pattern* means a model from which many things of the same kind and shape can be made, like houses which look the same, or shoes made alike, or a number of lorries all of the same size and shape, though perhaps of different colours. A sentence-pattern is therefore a model for sentences which will be of the same shape and construction although made up of different words.

A very useful sentence-pattern in English is :—

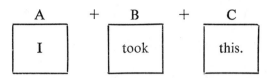

A   +   B   +   C

| I | took | this. |

In that pattern, the sentence is in three parts, and the word-order of the parts is always the same :—

At the beginning : A noun, or words like a noun	*in the middle* a verb	*after the verb* a noun or words like a noun
I Kazi Two of the men The woman and her husband	took will not buy tried to make refused to take	this the other one a wooden box a small lorry

Each division of the pattern may contain one word or it may contain a group of words stuck together in a phrase ; and it is possible to change the words or phrases in each division many times and so make hundreds of sentences. There are $4 \times 4 \times 4 = 64$ sentences in the example given above.

3. Notice how each part of the pattern is changed, step by step, in this example :—

(*a*) I   like   this one.
(*b*) Kazi   likes   this one.
(*c*) Kazi   made   this one.
(*d*) You   made   the other one.
(*e*) You   saw   the other one.

39

It is a useful exercise to make similar changes in another sentence-pattern. Try this one :—

Did | Kazi | buy | one ?

4. The chief difficulty in learning a new language is the trouble of changing from the sentence-patterns which you are used to in your own language to the sentence-patterns of the new language. Learning new words is easy, for that is only a question of simple memory and the building up of ' links ' ; but it is clearly necessary to teach the sentence-patterns of English, and to make them a habit, as early as possible. The student can easily learn large numbers of new words after he has left school, but he needs to know the sentence-patterns into which they can be fitted. That is why, in this book, more importance is given to the learning of patterns than to the learning of large numbers of new words.

5. Taking only simple sentences, and omitting double sentences like :—

    i. One of the men told me that
    ii. he was ill.

the sentence-patterns of English can be arranged in seven groups. The patterns in each group can be changed in many ways (chiefly by adding new parts), but the main shape of the pattern remains. These seven groups are :—

(1) *Two-part patterns* :   He / laughed.
    The poor old lion / went away on three legs.
(2) *Three-part patterns* :
    Daud / wrote / a book.
    You / have never seen / a lion with three legs.
(3) *Four-part patterns* :
    He / gave / me / a book.
    Learning sentence-patterns / will encourage / young students / to make long sentences.

(4) *Patterns with 'There'* : There are / seven.
(5) *Questions beginning with a Verb* :
   Has / he / done it ?
   Will / any of them / come to this house ?
(6) *Questions beginning with an asking-word* :
   When / did / Kazi / do it ?
   What / will / the richest man / say to me ?
(7) *Commands or Requests* :
                  Go away ! /
   Please don't take / the other one.

6. Out of 100 English sentences, 97 will be in the form of statements ; and of the statement sentence-patterns the three-part pattern is the most frequently used :—

   Daud / wrote / a book.
      I / like / this.
   My brother / isn't / a policeman.

Next in order of importance comes the pattern which begins with *There* :— There are three books on the table.

These two sentence-patterns are in the first rank of importance and must therefore be taught and drilled very early and very thoroughly.

In this drill, because the pupil learns by saying and doing things himself, the teacher's object will be, not to make statements of his own all the time, but to get the pupils to make statements. This is done by asking questions :—

Teacher : What is that ? *Pupil* : That is a red book.
Question patterns must therefore be taught at the same time as statement patterns.

For the same reason (in order to make the *pupils* do things) command patterns will be necessary as soon as the pupils have to learn verbs.

41

For these reasons, the early stages of teaching English must include :—

      i. Three-part statement patterns ;

     ii. The *There* pattern ;

    iii. Question patterns ;

and   iv. Command patterns.

7.   We have noticed that language is not made up of single words, but of words stuck together in groups. These groups also fall into patterns each of which is built upon a structural word :—

in the box	a ton *of* . . .
in the room	a pint of . . .
outside the room	a cupful of . . .
behind the trees	a pocketful of . . .

I know
- *what* to do
- where to go
- which one to buy
- whom to ask

These are phrase-patterns, and they are just as important and useful as sentence-patterns. They should be most carefully and thoroughly drilled in speech and in listening before the pupils are made to read them from the reading-book.

As the work proceeds, the teacher will collect in his own private notebook the most useful phrase-patterns. Some of them may be printed on brown paper and placed in the classroom, as they occur in the classwork. Such collections will include phrase-patterns of the following shapes among others, as they occur in the teaching :—

(*a*)	(*b*)
on the table	a lot of it
in the next house	a small quantity of it
under his foot	a good deal of it
across the road	plenty of it

(c) **a** lot of them 　　(d) **a** piece of it
　　 a small number of them 　　 **a** lump of it
　　 many of them 　　 **a** heap of it
　　 very few of them 　　 **a** drop of it

(e) **a** pair of them 　　(f) want to ⎫
　　 a set of them 　　 wish to ⎪
　　 a heap of them 　　 like to ⎬ do it
　　 a handful of them 　　 promise **to** ⎪
　　　　　　　　　　　　　 am going to ⎭

(g) **a** long list of time-phrases :
　　 to-day
　　 yesterday 　　　　　　　 on the ⎫ third
　　 the day before yesterday before the ⎬ of
　　 the next day 　　　　　　 after the ⎭ January
　　 next week

　　　 ⎧ five minutes past six 　 a long time ⎫
　 at ⎨ six o'clock 　　　　　　 some time ⎬ ago
　　　 ⎩ a quarter past two 　　 four days ⎪
　　　　　　　　　　　　　　 three days ⎭

These are only examples : many more will be found
in the ordinary course of classwork, and every good
classroom will always have three or four sheets of
them hanging on the walls.

8. It was pointed out in Chapter II that the
English language is constructed upon three principles :
two of these—word-order and structural words—
explain the shapes of sentence-patterns and phrase-
patterns. This should be pointed out to the pupils as
each pattern is learned, for mistakes in word-order and
in the use of structural words are the cause of most
'common errors'. In the higher classes, the details
of each kind of pattern will be carefully examined :—
　　It went *by post*. 　 *by post* = preposition + noun
　　It starts *by pressing a button*.

43

by pressing = preposition + *-ing* form + object
a button

9. To summarize this Chapter :

(1) Different languages have different sentence-patterns and phrase-patterns ; the chief difficulty in learning a new language is the difficulty of replacing the patterns of the mother-tongue by the patterns of the new language.

(2) Patterns are based on word-order and on structural words. The sentence-patterns of most use in English are : the three-part pattern ; the *There* pattern ; question patterns ; and command patterns.

Points to think about and discuss

1. Collect some of the sentence-patterns most commonly used in your own language. Do they agree, or disagree, with their translations into English ?

2. Give the sentence-patterns in your own language for these English patterns :—

    i. He / told / me / to do it.

    ii. There are / seven clever girls / in that room.

    iii. It is / about half-past four.

3. In the same way, compare these English patterns with their translations into your own language :—

    i. I know / what to do.
                where to go.

    ii. He does it / once a day.
                 twice a week.
                 three times a year.

    iii. I use it / for sharpening pencils.
                for cleaning my teeth.
                for sitting on.

4. Give three more examples of each of these pat-

terns ; notice the difference between them (with *to* ; without *to*) :—

    i. Ask / somebody / to do it.
    ii. Make / somebody / do it.

For the practical teacher

1. From the beginning, the pupils must be given much practice in collocations (groups of words stuck together in a set pattern). This can be done by asking them to change one part of a pattern at a time. For example, even young beginners can alter the numbers in

    One/ of the boys/ went home.
    Two . . . . . .   Three . . . . . .   etc.

They may then alter the noun :—

    One / of the boys / went home.
          of the men
          of the lions   etc.

The pupils may then be asked to prepare movable strips to fit into the pattern :—

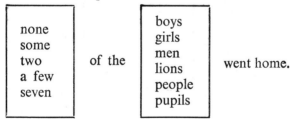

| none
some
two
a few
seven | of the | boys
girls
men
lions
people
pupils | went home. |

2. Similar strips can be made for structural verbs :

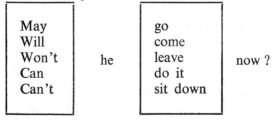

| May
Will
Won't
Can
Can't | he | go
come
leave
do it
sit down | now ? |

3. The easiest form for the future tense in English is *to be going to . . . .*

I'm		do it	tomorrow
He's	going to	come here	next week
She's		go away	at five o'clock
They're			the day after tomorrow
			in June

4. Question patterns, and the Statement patterns which answer them, can be practised on a picture which can easily be drawn on the blackboard :—

Let a square = a house ; ⚲ = a man ; ⚲ = a woman

The pupils ask questions, and answer them :

How many men are there   in the house ?
                                outside the house ?
                                on the top of the house ? *etc.*

There is one man on the top of the house. *etc.*

5. Pupils can prepare cards showing different

parts of a pattern, and under orders from the class, move about to form sentences :—

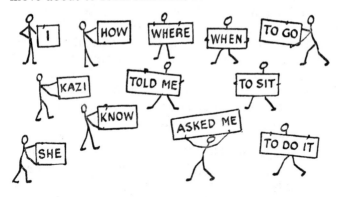

CHAPTER VI

SPEECH

1. If a headmaster, or an inspector of schools, wishes to judge a teacher's ability to teach English, he will always ask to hear a lesson in which most of the time is given up to talking by the pupils rather than a lesson spent entirely on reading from the reading-book. The weak teacher relies too much on the reading-book ; in a reading lesson the teacher does not have to work very hard himself ; the pupils are quiet and still, and all the material for the lesson is on the printed page. But in a reading lesson it is almost impossible to tell whether the backward pupils are paying attention all the time ; the lesson is very often only a string of little individual lessons for particular pupils while the rest of the class are doing nothing, or very little. The children are not active,

and therefore their minds are not making those strong ' links ' which are the foundation of memory. There is no drill ; and most important of all, there is no fun, no interest, no enjoyment in the lesson.

It is a bad teacher who complains that ' the reading-book is not long enough ; I want more pages of reading to be added to it in order to fill the time.'

But in a good lesson in which most of the time is spent encouraging the *pupils* to speak, and not in talk by the teacher, every pupil has to try to answer every question, for if he does not, he may be caught when the teacher calls upon him. There is a great deal of activity—pointing, acting, speaking—and the backward pupil can easily be picked out, for he is unable to take his part. In a reading lesson he simply keeps quiet and looks at his book, hoping that he will not be called upon. And as often as not, his hopes are fulfilled, and he gets through the lesson without learning anything.

The argument put forward in this book is that speaking is the necessary groundwork for every other stage of learning English ; that by speaking the pupil will be able to make all the links and associations in his mind required to fix new words ; and that by speaking he will build up the habit of using the correct sentence-patterns and phrase-patterns. And finally, that, in the early stages at least, the pupil should read only those words and patterns with which he is already familiar through speech. He should never be asked to read, or to write, anything which he has not first thoroughly learned through speaking it.

Lessons in speaking, therefore, must on no account be omitted or cut down ; they are the most important part of the work.

2. The first difficulty that the teacher will meet with—and it occurs throughout the course—is that the

sounds of English are not the same as the sounds of the pupil's own language. There are, of course, many sounds which occur both in the mother-tongue and in English, but there are others which are found in one but not in the other.

The *st* sound is used in many languages, but always in the middle, or at the end of a word. In English, it occurs at the beginning of words as well. To many learners, this is strange and they find great difficulty in beginning a word with the sound *st*. They cannot say *stay ;* they say *estay*, so as to get the *st* into the middle instead of at the beginning.

There are many other difficult sounds : *w v th l* and *r* are examples.

To meet difficulties such as these, the first step is to train the pupils, not to say these difficult sounds themselves, but to hear them. In this work, as in all English lessons, the first stage is listening. The teacher, therefore, must first of all drill himself in saying these sounds correctly ; this he can do by giving some private study to the sounds of English.

3. The sounds of English may be arranged in three groups :—

vowels, double vowels or diphthongs, and consonants.

The consonants are :—

*b*ud, *p*ip, *d*ot, *t*op, *k*ick, *g*o, *f*or, *l*ong, *m*an, *n*o, *h*appy, *v*ery, *w*ell, *r*oll, *s*o, *z*ero, *sh*e, *th*in, *th*en, si*ng*er, plea*s*ure, *y*es.

4. There are twelve vowel sounds in English : six short, five long, and a very short 'neutral' vowel :—

Short vowels : h*i*d l*e*d h*a*d h*o*d h*u*t h*oo*d

Long vowels : h*ee*d h*ar*d h*oar*d wh*o*'d h*ear*d

The very short neutral vowel is very much used in English although never in any position of importance.

49

It is heard best in the very short ă of ă book, ă man ; and as the last sound in paint*er*, bett*er*.

5. Double vowels or diphthongs are also common in English. A diphthong is the result produced by melting two vowels together. Listen to the two vowel sounds which are joined together to form one syllable in :—

$$d(ay) = (a + ee) \qquad b(oy) = (aw + ee)$$

Here is a list of the most frequently used diphthongs. It is not complete because it is not the object of this book to teach the sounds of English. The list is given here only for illustration and for practice. Try to recognize the two vowel sounds which are hidden in each diphthong :—

d(*ay*)   b(*oy*)   n(*o*)   h(*ere*)   m(*y*)   th(*ere*)
c(*ow*)   m(*ore*)   h(*ue*)

6. Some of these vowels, consonants and diphthongs may be strange to the pupil because they do not appear in his own language. He will be tempted to substitute for them sounds from his own speech.

The following sounds have been found to be particularly difficult for speakers of languages other than English :—

i. the short ă as in c*ă*p, c*ă*t, r*ă*t. Very few languages possess this short sound, although many have a sound very much like it, but longer.

ii. the short ă̆ is often confused with the short ĕ ; as in m*ĕ*t, l*ĕ*t, s*ĕ*t, so that *cat* is often pronounced *cet*.

The difference is seen in these pairs of words :—

mat, met ;   sat, set ;   bad, bed ;   man, men.

iii. the two sounds of *th* as in *thin* and *then*.

In the first place, the pupil finds difficulty

50

in *hearing* the difference ; secondly, he has trouble in pronouncing the difference himself ; and thirdly, in trying to say the two sounds, he gets them mixed up with *s*, *d*, and *t*, so that instead of saying *thin* he says *sin* or *tin*, and instead of saying *then*, he says *den*.

The first sound, *th* in *thin*, can be made by biting the tongue between the teeth and blowing air out at the same time, though with practice it can be made, as English people make it, without biting the tongue.

The second sound *th* in *then*, is also made by biting the tongue between the teeth but the air is blown out with less force ; it is used, instead, to make a deep noise in the throat-box. These sounds may be used for practice :—

(*a*) *th* in *thin* : (Say the words both across and upwards :—

thin	think	thank	thick
sin	sink	sank	sick
tin	tink	tank	tick

(*b*) *th* in *then* :

| then | though | that | there |
| send | sow | sat | |

7. Some speakers find it hard to hear or to say the difference between *r* and *l*. They should practise these pairs of words :—

| rap | red | rip | road |
| lap | led | lip | load |

The *l* sound is the only case in English in which the sound comes out of the mouth by passing on *both* sides of the tongue.

8. The *ly* at the end of English adverbs is a very short sound. Put the stress on the first syllable of the word :—

*quick*lĭ (not quick*lee*) *slow*lĭ *hard*lĭ

51

9. These things are hard to explain to young people because it is almost impossible to describe a noise by making an explanation in words. The same is true of colours and smells. You cannot describe *blue* in words—you can only show an example of a piece of blue cloth or paper. In teaching sounds which are new, because they do not occur in the pupils' own language, it is possible to do three things :

(*a*) to give an example ; (*b*) to tell the pupils where the sound is made (in the throat, with the teeth, or with the lips) ; and (*c*) to tell them how it is made.

10. For both vowels and consonants there are two kinds of sounds :—

(i) voiced sounds in which air is passed through the vocal chords so that you can feel the chords vibrating if you put your finger on the outside of the throat. Try the word *some*.

(ii) voiceless sounds in which the vocal chords are not used.

Try the word *hiss*.

11. Some sounds are like explosions : *p*, *b*, *k*.
Some sounds are made in the nose : *m*, *ng*
Sometimes the tip of the tongue is made to vibrate very rapidly, as in *arrr*.
Sometimes the air is blown out through a small passage : *f*, *v*, *sh*

12. It is useful to take a mirror and watch your own mouth as you say certain sounds. Do this with the long vowel sounds in *heed* and *hard*, and in *who'd* and *heard* ; watch how your mouth changes.

Watch what happens in these cases :—

(*a*) What does T H E spell ? Say it, and look in the mirror.

(b) Now say quickly, *thĕ man*. The long sound of *ee* in *the* disappears, and its place is taken by a very short, very weak sound. Notice that this very weak sound is very important in English. Try to hear it in *paint, painter*; *wet, wetter*. This is the 'neutral vowel' (see para. 4).

Similar exercises may be practised with other sounds.

13. The most valuable lessons in speech training for beginners are those which deal with the vowels and the double-vowels or diphthongs; they have been called the flesh and blood of English speech, covering the bony skeleton of its consonants. Many of them, standing alone, make English words :—

are, or, err, owe, I, ear, air ;

Some of them are heard at the ends of words. For example :—

the short ĭ as in hĭd :— city, money, ready, happy ;

Some of them never occur at the end of a word :—

the short ă of hăd, the short ŏ of hŏp, and the short ŭ of mŭd.

14. *ng* never comes at the beginning of an English word, although it is found at the beginning of many words in other languages. In English, it comes in the middle or at the end :—

si*ng*er, si*ng* ; notice the difference between *singer* and *longer*.

No English word ends in an *h sound*, although many words have a last *letter h* :— tooth, dish, laugh.

The teacher should watch carefully for examples of how sounds are used in English, and how they are not used, comparing what he finds with the sounds of his own language.

15. The pronunciation of words is not only a

matter of sounds ; it includes also differences in accent or stress. Some words have the heavier stress on the first part of the word :—

> STAtion, LOrry, ANswer, REAding, ORder, MORNing ;

and other words have the heavier stress on the second part :—

> explAIN, oBEY, reSULT, misTAKE, aGAIN.

Those words contain two syllables ; the word *boy* contains only one ; *happily* has three ; *unhappily* has four syllables.

A good example of the difference between syllables is seen in the word *banana*. In that word, the first and last syllables have the ' neutral vowel ' but the middle syllable is heavy and long.

More attention is paid to stress in English than in any other language ; that is why foreigners often find it difficult to understand an Englishman's speech, and ask him to ' Please speak more slowly.' In quick speech, the accented syllables are so strong that they almost drown the others. Try this sentence :—

> I think that that 'that' that that pupil has just spoken is wrong.

16. The question of stress arises very early in the teaching of English, almost in the first lessons :—

> *What's this* ? It's a WINdow. Is it BROken ?
> TAke a BOOk out of the BOX.

In sentence-patterns and phrase-patterns the stress often falls in the same place :—

> He told me   WHAT to do
>   WHERE to go
>   WHY he did it
>   WHEN to begin

This point must be borne in mind when drilling patterns ; and at all times the good teacher will see that his pupils make the *English* sounds, and not the sounds of their mother-tongue which are nearly, but not quite, the same.

Points to think about and discuss

1. A little child learning his own language does not get any lessons about vowels, diphthongs, or consonants. How, then, does he learn to move his throat, tongue and lips in the correct way ? Consider this with reference to your own language.

Similarly, such a child does not get any drill in sounds ; why is it necessary to give sound drills to pupils learning English as a foreign language ?

2. Make a list of sounds which occur in your own language, but do not occur in English. Compare your list with the lists made by your friends.

3. Do these English sounds occur in your own language ?

a. the ' neutral vowel ' as in paint*e*r, *a*live

b. *st* at the beginning of a word, as in *stop*

c. *th* as in *think*

d. *th* as in *though*

e. *oi* at the beginning, as in *oil*

f. the sound represented by the letter *y* in *yard*

4. Look in the mirror and say *we* in order to see how the *w* sound is made. These words end with the letter *w* ; do they end with the *sound* you just made in saying *we* :—

new, now, raw, law ?

5. All these words end with the letter *d* when written ; do they all end with the *d* sound when spoken ?

robbed	picked	answered	asked	finished
helped	called	liked	noticed	listened
passed	paid	stopped	seemed	talked

6. With the help of someone whose English pronunciation is very good, practise these sounds :—

(a)	bath	bathe	(b)	boat	both
	mouth	mouths		true	threw
	breath	breathe		taught	thought
(c)	cloth	clothes	(d)	tanks	thanks
	tooth	smooth		den	then
	south	southerly		they	day

7. Say quickly, reading across (not down) :—

a long island	a longer island
a strong man	a stronger man
a young man	a younger man

Is there any difference in the sounds represented in print by *ng* ?

For the practical teacher

1. The falling tone is the most common in English : therefore always use it when teaching a new word :—

2. (i) When the Present Continuous Tense is being taught, it is absolutely essential that the words should be spoken *at the same moment* as the action is done. It is therefore wrong to teach *I'm laughing* by this method.

(ii) the spoken forms should be used :—

I'm/ You're/ He's/ She's/ We're/ They're *walking.*

also

I've/ You've/ He's/ We've/ They've *opened the door.*

3. Do not allow your pupils to forget the correct sound even when it is hidden in the English

spelling :—

 a. be,bee,these,people,sea,field,key,machine,police
 b. ship,busy,women,minute
 c. ten,led,bread,friend,said,says
 d. car,father,laugh,France
 e. or,broad,taught,caught,all,talk,water
 f. fun,come,done,mother,does,blood

4. Singing and whispering the vowel sounds are both very good forms of exercise.

5. Two experiments :—

 i. Say *bat*.   Now say *battle*.
    Can you feel the air passing *both* sides of the tongue for the *l* sound ?

 ii. Take a piece of paper about eight inches long and one inch wide.   Hold it so that one end hangs about one inch from your mouth.

    Say *pop*.   What happens ? The paper shows that air comes out of your mouth very strongly, in two puffs.
    Try these :— *bob,   tot,   kick*

In some consonants the air does not come out in a puff, but in a stream.   Try these with the strip of paper :—

  if   live   teeth   (f   v   th)

6. A more difficult exercise is to take the vowel sounds given in paragraph 4 of this Chapter and put different consonants *after* them :—

(*short*) : hid head (*hed*) had hod hood hut
Now change the *d* to *t* and drop the *h* :—

  it   et   at   ot   oot   ut

Change the *t* to *p* :—

  ip   ep   ap   op   oop   up

(Useful consonants for this purpose are *t p m* and *d*.

57

CHAPTER VII

READING

1. According to the conditions in the school, the work of teaching the pupils to read in English may appear to begin from any of three starting-points :—

a. the pupils may be able to read their own language in English print ;

b. the pupils may be able to read their own language, but not in English print ;

c. they may not be able to read at all.

As a matter of fact, there is but one starting-point and one aim ; the only difference between the three kinds of pupils just mentioned is that the first kind will be able to cover the first steps very rapidly indeed ; the second class of pupil will go a little more slowly ; and the third class will require the longest time of all.

The aim of the teacher is to get his pupils as quickly as possible over the period in which each printed symbol is looked at for its shape, and to arrive at the stage when the pupil looks at words and phrases, *for their meaning*, almost without noticing the shapes of the separate letters.

2. When a good reader is at work, he does not look at letters, nor even at words, one by one, however quickly ; he takes in the meaning of two, three, or four words at a time, in a single moment. Watch carefully the eyes of a person who is reading, and it will be seen that they do not travel smoothly along the lines of print, but they move by jumps separated by very short stops. The eyes of a very good reader move quickly, taking long jumps and making very short halts ; the eyes of a poor reader move more

slowly, taking only short jumps and stopping longer at each halt. Sometimes, when he meets a difficulty, they even go backwards to see again what has already been looked at once.

The teacher's task is therefore clear : it is to train his pupils to take in several words at a glance (one ' eye-jump ') and to remove the necessity for going backwards to read something a second time.

2. This shows at once that letter-by-letter, or syllable-by-syllable, or word-by-word reading, with the finger pointing to the word, carefully fixing each one in turn, is wrong. It is wrong because such a method ties the pupil's eye down to a very short jump, and the aim is to train for the long jump. Moreover, a very short jump is too short to provide any meaning or sense ; and it will be found that having struggled with three or four words separately, the pupil has to look at them again, all together and in one group, in order to get the meaning of the whole phrase.

3. Of course, at the very beginning, the pupil is compelled to look at each printed letter separately in order to be certain of its shape ; but he must be helped through this stage as quickly as possible. He must be taught to see, *not*

It   is   on   the   table.   *but*
          (It is)   (on the table.)

4. If the pupils cannot read at all and must begin at the beginning, the English letters should not be taught one by one, or in alphabetical order, or by their names (ay,bee,cee,dee). Even the first steps should be in easy groups ; and this work may often be linked closely with the work of pronouncing the English sounds. It is true that one English letter may stand for more than one sound (*c* in *cancel*) but this

difficulty will not arise in the very first lessons, for it is possible to find groups which enable the pupil to connect the printed shape with the sound it commonly represents ; or groups of shapes. For example :—

mill	fill	kill	pill	till
mile	file	tile	pile	

and the child will soon learn, even without special teaching,

ton, tone ; can, cane ; mill, mile

or groups such as *eep* and *ight* :—

sleep	deep,	keep,	sheep
night,	fight,	right,	light

5. In this way the child is led from the single letter to the group ; that is, from letters to eye-jumps which, though short, are longer than one letter-space. The next step is obviously a very short sentence-pattern. The child can easily take in at one glance short patterns such as :—

What's this ? What's that ? It's a book.

or short phrase-patterns such as :—

at four o'clock ; next week ; in the box.

6. It will be noticed that this method of training the pupils to read groups by ' Look and Say ' brings us back to the same principles that are to be used in the speaking lessons—sentence- and phrase-patterns, not separate words. It follows that the lessons in the first reading-books can agree very closely with the first lessons in speaking. To this may be added the very great advantage that if the pupil finds he has to read only what he knows quite well already through speech, all his difficulties are reduced to only one—the recognition of the appearance of words in print.

Here lies a trap for the weak teacher. It is easy, and it saves a lot of trouble, if the teacher gives up trying to arrange speaking lessons, and turns every lesson into reading from the ' Reader ' ; most of the class is quiet, the teacher himself has very little to do, and lessons pass quickly. But the pupils fail to learn English. The teacher who receives the pupils into the next class the following year complains that 'their ground-work is weak ' ; and that is quite true, for the weak teacher has forgotten all about the importance of listening, of making strong links between the word (or phrase) and the object or action it describes. The pupils have had none of that necessary practice which they can get *only* by speaking. For this reason many headmasters and headmistresses put their best English teacher, not in charge of the top class, but in charge of the beginners' class, because a good teacher will never make the very bad mistake of turning every lesson into a reading or writing lesson, but will spend most of his time on the speaking lessons. He knows that reading and writing will give the pupils very little trouble (and they will not make ' mistakes ') if everything they have to read and to write is first well drilled through speech.

7. Because the work in reading is so closely connected with, and follows step by step, the work in speech, the objects and pictures chosen for the speaking-lessons must appear in the reading-book. The objects and pictures must therefore be chosen to serve two purposes : (*a*) they must be suitable for teaching the objects, actions, questions, answers, statements, and orders which make up the work in speech, and (*b*) they must also be suitable for teaching the connection between the spoken sound and printed symbol.

This is the value of the ' Picture Dictionary ' referred to on page 27, which forms part of both speaking and reading lessons.

8. The objects drawn in a Picture Dictionary such as that used in the Oxford series are selected with three aims in mind :—

    a. to teach new words which shall be useful both in speech and in reading ;

    b. to give reading practice based on groups of sounds (vowels or consonants, or both) ;

    c. to illustrate particular letter-shapes.

For example, under *C* there are pictures of

cat	(short $\breve{a}$ sound)
car	(long $\bar{a}$ sound)
cow	(diphthong)
cock	(short $\breve{o}$ sound)
cup	(short $\breve{u}$ sound)
crying	(long $\bar{\imath}$ sound)
cooking	(middle *o* sound)

and also *ch*ur*ch*, ca*tch*ing, and *ch*air, for the *ch* sound in which the printed letter *c* takes part.

These words are all taught, in speech, in sentence-patterns :—

        Point to / the cat.

        Point to / the picture of / a cat.

        Show me /a cat.

        What's that ? It's a cat.

And these patterns appear again in the reading lessons.

9. The reading book and the pictures it contains are not the only materials which are used in teaching reading. Before the pupils are asked to read direct from the classbook, they will be given reading practice in many other ways, of which the following are examples :—

    i. Flash-cards. These are arranged in groups, and as the cards are held up, one by one, before the class, the pupils read them aloud :—

sing	wing	king	bring
walk	talk	chalk	stalk
pick	thick	brick	stick

ii. Word-building cards. Suitable words (they must be carefully selected on account of spelling difficulties) are put on the blackboard and cards showing endings are placed after each one, the class reading the result :—

hold   learn

throw   fight

ER

sing   read

shoot   buy

ING

play   push

Word-building cards may also be used for plain reading drill :

st	c	l	sl
t	g	wr	cr
	OP		OAT		ONG		EEP
h	b	str	d
sh	fl	s	sh

iii. Order-cards. Simple orders (already known to the pupils through the speaking lessons) are printed on the cards, or on a roll, and are flashed before the class. The pupils have to read the order and obey it in silence :—

Open your books.   *Raise your right hand.*
Touch the desk.   *Point to the window.*

This work is very valuable because it gives training in the quick reading and understanding of a whole group of words, with no time for silent translation.

10. In hints ' for the practical teacher ' in Chapter I of this book, it has been suggested that the pupils

63

should collect and bring to the class all kinds of pictures, especially small ones. These, too, can be used for reading practice before the class-reader is opened. A sentence may be printed on the blackboard with a missing word ; the pupil has to supply a suitable picture to fill the space :—

My father is a   I have a

The is near the shop.

11. It is not necessary to spend much time on such questions as :

Should the pupils in the class be made to read aloud all together ?

Should the teacher first read the lesson aloud to the class as a pattern ?

Which is more important, reading aloud or silent reading ?

All these things have their uses, in the proper place and at the proper time. When using flash-cards, the class may sometimes read the card all together, and sometimes they will put up their hands but the teacher will call upon only one pupil.

Sometimes the teacher will read a story to the class, or give a pattern reading, just for a change.

If the speaking has been well done, there will be much silent reading by the pupils themselves, even out of school hours, because they will find that the reading-book contains only what they have already learned very thoroughly.

The good teacher never ties himself down to one method ; he uses many different methods all in one lesson. That is why his lessons are interesting, happy, and successful.

12. As the pupils progress in reading, both the material and the lesson methods change. In the earlier stages the object is to give a perfect mastery of the most useful sentence- and phrase-patterns, and to build up a vocabulary of the most useful words. In the later stages the aim is to provide reading practice for understanding. This cannot be done until the pupils are well drilled in all the common tenses and have a vocabulary of at least 500 words ; for the main difficulties in the higher classes are new words and new constructions. To meet both of these, there must be oral work ; new words are examined and used in different settings ; new constructions are drilled in the same way as before, by patterns and tables. There will be tests of different kinds.

But the golden rule remains the same throughout the Course : Be in no hurry to turn to the Reader ; time spent on speaking practice is time saved. Only the bad teacher finishes the Reader before the end of the year.

Points to think about and discuss

1. Young pupils sometimes ' lose the place ' in the reading lesson, and in order to stop this, and to make them pay more attention, the teacher orders the class to point to each word as it is read. In view of the aim of the lesson, which is to teach the reading of word-groups, is this a good thing for teachers to do ? Give reasons for your answer.

65

2. Some people move their lips when they are reading to themselves. Why do they do this ? What effect has it on the speed of their reading ?

Very young pupils may be permitted to do it if they wish ; how does it help them ?

Older students should be discouraged from doing it : why ?

3. Some languages are written exactly as they are spoken ; English is not. Prove this by taking these words as your examples :—

(a) patient ; shall   (b) off ; cough
(c) boat ; both   (d) through ; threw

4. Consider the two letters joined : *ng*. In some words, this group stands for only one sound : sing, ring.

In other words it stands for two sounds, *ng-g* : finger, England.

In which of these words does *ng* stand for one sound, and in which does it stand for two sounds ?

sing	singer	singing	single	young
long	strong	longer	longest	angry
bringing	hang	songbird	strongest	

5. Look at the English vowel sounds given in paragraph 4 of Chapter VI. Say which vowel is used in each of these words—as underlined :—

p*ie*ce	p*ea*ce	f*ee*t	mach*ine*
n*e*ver	b*u*ry	s*ai*d	
c*a*rt	c*a*rve	f*a*ther	
m*a*d	h*a*nd	l*a*mp	
*i*f	d*i*d	sh*i*p	

6. Do your own lips move (a) when you read to yourself ? (b) when you write ? If you are not sure, ask a friend to watch you, when you are thinking of something else.

When you are reading silently, do you ' hear ' the words inside your head ? Does the same thing happen when you write ?

Do you see any connection between this and the importance of speech ?

7. If you were an inspector of schools, what material would you expect to see hung upon the walls of a classroom where the pupils had just completed the First Year of the English Course ?

8. Prepare a wall-chart to be hung in the classroom entitled ' The Letter A '. showing the different sounds the letter can represent. Under each sound put three words as examples :—

The Letter A.			
short	*long*	*ay*	*aw*
hat	father	made	ball
—	—	—	—
—	—	—	—

9. Consider how you would use these groups for flash-card work. (These lists will be very useful to you in your teaching.)

way	row	out	test	not	felt	ought
pay	grow	about	nest	knot	melt	bought
stay	know	scout	rest	blot	belt	fought
say	slow	shout	best	shot	smelt	thought
may	low	stout	west	hot		brought
lay	flow			got		
day	blow			dot		

sight	jumps	drop	damp	worn	green
night	humps	crop	lamp	torn	seen
fight	lumps	stop	stamp	horn	fifteen
right	pumps	top	camp	corn	queen
bright				born	between
might					

gain	seaman	bell	dream	oil
again	madman	fell	scream	boil
chain	fireman	tell	cream	soil
plain	horseman	shell	stream	spoil
rain	watchman	smell	steam	
stain	workman	sell		
main	woman	well		
pain	shopman			
train	chairman			

ink	thank	rock	dash	size
think	blank	lock	flash	prize
drink	rank	knock	fresh	freeze
sink	drank	block	flesh	breeze
wink	sank	clock	dish	
	tank	shock	fish	

needle	circle	able	smoke	age
candle	cycle	double	joke	cage
handle	uncle	noble	spoke	page
bundle		tumble	broke	wage
idle		tremble	awoke	
		bubble		
		table		

village	head
manage	dead
voyage	bread
cottage	instead
message	thread

For the practical teacher

1. Charts and flash-cards can be used together.

Chart				Flash-cards	
I	have	a	pencil	MY	THIS IS
I	have	a	book		
He	has	a	bag	HIS	IS THIS
She	has	a	box		
We	have	a	football	HER	THAT ISN'T
They	have	a	knife	OUR	HAS HE

i. The flash-cards (MY, etc.) may be placed over the word *a* on the chart.

ii. The flash-cards (THIS IS, etc.) may be placed over the words *I Have, etc.*, with or without the (MY) flash-cards.

2. Pupils may be given flash-cards and told to arrange themselves in sentences according to instructions, and the class read the sentences so formed :—

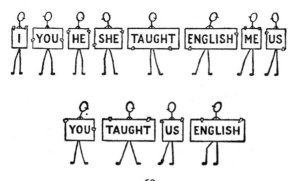

69

3. Silent orders are good fun and good reading practice. The teacher puts on the blackboard (with the board turned away from the pupils so that they cannot see his writing) :

1. Open the door and touch your head.
2. Hold your left ear and walk round the table.

He then turns the blackboard to the class and names two pupils to obey the written orders, in silence.

4. Pupils can cut words out of newspapers and keep them in their desks. With these they make sentences to fit pictures.

They are running   to the lorry

The words can be kept in trays (see para. 20, Chapter XI.)

5. A chart can be made of sentences from different pages of the Reader. The class has to find the picture to which the sentence belongs. (An example is given in Lesson 37, *First Year English ; Part Two ; Reading.*)

The same exercise can be done with large scale pictures in front of the class, the teacher writing the sentences on the blackboard.

6. As much as possible of the work of preparing charts and flash-cards should be done by the pupils themselves. The effort is of very great value to them. There is more about this in Chapter XI.

CHAPTER VIII

WRITING

1. The importance of written work is not the same for all pupils ; there must be some written work in all classes because it provides forms of exercise which are most useful in fixing vocabulary and sentence-patterns ; but its practical value is very small for pupils who receive only two or three years of instruction in English.

Many teachers give too much time to it ; a writing lesson is restful ; the effort which the teacher has to put into it is much less than that required for a lesson in speech or even in reading ; the pupil, too, works at a much slower pace. But written work cannot be compared with oral work as a means of making solid progress.

Give writing its due ; but, in the first three years, do not allow it to take up time which should be given to more useful kinds of English work.

2. Written work is to be considered from two quite different points of view : (a) as penmanship or simple handwriting, and (b) as a form of exercise in learning the language. We will first deal with the question of penmanship.

The writing of the English letters, and writing them in combinations, may be taught in the lessons on the mother-tongue, if that is printed in English lettering. Or it may have to be taught separately. In either case it is not an easy thing for a small pupil to learn, because it requires very fine control of the small muscles of the fingers and the wrist. A child has great difficulty in controlling even his larger muscles—watch him trying to throw a stone at an object ; it is much harder for him to learn to perform correctly very small actions such as drawing the shape of a letter.

Training in penmanship should therefore proceed by easy steps.

  i. Fairly large movements, using the finger in a tray of sand, or chalk on brown paper : lines of various lengths and directions :—

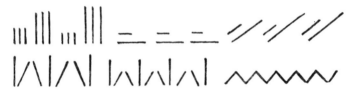

  ii. Script writing : small letters but large in size, arranged in groups similar in shape :

o a c e d b g q p

m n h r f j l i t y u

w v x z k

s

Each stroke must be continuous ; the body of
the letter occupies one space (two lines), the
stem one more space above, the tail one more
space below. Letters must be upright and
therefore parallel ; spacing equal.

iii. The spacing of letters is important for the neat
appearance of the writing, but it gives children
much difficulty. In forming words, letters
must be as close as possible without touching ;
and the spaces between words should be even,
each one large enough for a capital O to be
fitted into it, that is to say at least two full
letter-spaces. At first the rule may be,
' Letters close ; words apart.'

iv. Capital letters should not be taught until all
the small letters have been learned. The
capitals also arrange themselves in groups :—
Round capitals (each filling one circle) :

OQCGD

Square capitals (each filling one square) :

HNMTZAXUVW

Half square capitals (each filling half a
square) :

EFLKYIJ

Half circle :

SPBR

73

v. Later, the letters may be joined by giving each small letter a little tail as a ' joiner ' ; but this should not be attempted until the beginning of the third year.

vi. The positions of the body, arm, head, and paper must be carefully watched at all times : body upright and parallel to the desk ; head bent, eyes 12″ from the paper ; edge of the paper parallel to the edge of the desk. The hand rests lightly on the end of the little finger and the side of the wrist.

The pencil should be held lightly, in such a way that the first finger can be moved up and down (on and off the pencil) by itself. It should be possible to draw the pencil gently from the child's grip ; if that is not possible, the pencil is being held with too much strength.

On no account use slates. They ruin any lesson in writing, for they are hard, heavy, and slippery. Also they are very dirty and unhealthy.

3. We may now turn to the consideration of writing as a form of exercise in teaching the language.

Writing is a much slower process than either speaking or reading. The child's mind can move at its own pace ; he has plenty of time to think over what he is doing. As he writes he thinks about the sentence both as a whole and in its separate parts. For these reasons, the writing exercise has a powerful effect on the child's mind and provides a very good way of fixing vocabulary, spelling, and patterns of all kinds. Notice that writing is not a means of *teaching* these things ; it can only *fix* them after they have been learned.

4. Outside the lessons on penmanship, the first kind of writing exercise (which can be given as soon as the class Reader is used) is copying or transcription. The purpose of this exercise is to allow the pupil's mind to play round what has been taught in listening and speaking, and so fix it firmly. Writing does this because the movements of the muscles of the hand are now called in to help the ear, the eye, and the muscles and nerves of the throat and tongue. The ' look' and the ' feel ' of the word are used to help the memory. That applies equally well to the sentence-pattern and the phrase-pattern ; for the child should not be asked to write, in the first three years, anything that he does not already know thoroughly through speech and reading. ' Free Composition ' in which the child has to make up his own thoughts, has no place in the first three years. If it is used, it will only result in a large number of most discouraging mistakes.

Every new pattern, *after* it has been thoroughly learned, should be practised by transcription.

5. The second kind of writing exercise, which should not be introduced too early, is dictation. This is much more difficult than transcription, and it should *never* be given as a test to young beginners. It is a means of fixing what is already known, not a puzzle in which the teacher tries to defeat the pupil. A beginner should never be allowed to see, or to write, or to have time to think about a mistake.

Everything he writes must be easy for him because he is asked to write only those things which he already knows thoroughly.

Dictation which results in mistakes is very dangerous ; it does no good at all ; it does a very great deal of harm.

75

Dictation, when given within the limits just described, is a valuable exercise, because :—

i. It trains the ear to listen carefully to spoken English sounds ; in this, it helps both listening and speaking ;

ii. it uses the hand as well as the eye for practising the shapes of words ; and this is far better than oral spelling by the names of the letters (*ell,ee,tee,tee,ee,are,ess*) ;

iii. it fixes in the pupil's mind the divisions of each sentence-pattern, because the good teacher, when he dictates, will dictate division by division :—

My son Kazi / did not go away / until yesterday. These divisions are brought to the pupil's notice by sound, by appearance, and by muscular memory.

iv. Dictation uses ' the mind's eye'. In fact, it is a good preparation for the teacher to put a new word or phrase on the blackboard, and then, after teaching it thoroughly, tell the pupils to close their eyes and say it while looking at it ' in the dark, in the mind's eye'.

6. The third kind of writing exercise, still more difficult for beginners, is the writing of sentences on a given pattern, the words being chosen by the pupils. The first step, of course, is to ask for an alteration in only one division of the pattern :

i. How many / . . . ./ are there / on the table ?

ii. How many/ pieces of paper / are there/ . . . . ?

The pupils may then write a sentence of their own :

How many boys are there in this room ?

Practice of this kind can lead to quite long sentences, and even to short compositions ; but every sentence-pattern must be most carefully practised before the writing begins, and the pupils should not be asked to make more than one change at a time. The object is *to get it right*. A mistake is proof, not that the pupil has been lazy, but that the teacher has not given the class sufficient preparation.

7. The fourth kind of written exercise for the early stages is the writing of answers to given questions. This is one step beyond the pattern work described in paragraph 6, above. The question helps the pupil both with the words and with the pattern required for the answer. Here again, plenty of preparation is necessary to make sure that there are no mistakes.

This form of exercise can lead up to continuous composition in the form of writing out a story which has been told or read to the class. When the story is known, the leading questions are put on the blackboard and each one is answered orally. When the whole story has been completed in this way, without any writing except by the teacher, the questions may be left on the blackboard for the children to see, and, writing out their own answers, they find themselves writing out the story.

Very great care is necessary in the higher classes where ' free ' composition begins, because the pupil is forced first to think of ideas, and this he can do *only* in his own language. Free composition is therefore an exercise in very difficult translation, although the pupil may not actually speak aloud, or write, anything but English. This point is often forgotten, but it is the cause of nearly all the mistakes which students make in writing ' compositions'. The mistakes occur because the translation is too difficult for them.

For this reason, special kinds of preparation are needed for the composition lesson :—

    i. the pupil must be helped with his ideas ; this

is done by the oral preparation for the composition ;

ii. he must be helped to choose the right sentence-patterns in which to express those ideas ; this again is done in oral preparation.

Points to think about and discuss

1. Study your own handwriting under these heads :—

   i. Which letters are well shaped ? Which are badly shaped ? What is wrong with the bad letters ?

  ii. Is the spacing even ? Are there good spaces between words ?

 iii. How do you sit and hold your pen and the paper when you write ?

 iv. Do you hold your pen in the same way as other people ?

A teacher who writes badly himself cannot teach his pupils to write well.

2. In this and in previous Chapters there has been mention of brown paper. Probably your school will be unable to supply it. How will you obtain it ? Discuss methods with your friends.

3. If an American asked you to teach him your own language in three months, would you include writing ?

Give reasons for your answer.

4. If some villagers asked you to teach them some English in the evenings, would you include any writing ?

5. Some very good teachers advise that no writing at all should be attempted in the first six months of teaching English. Discuss this, and form your own opinion.

6. If, in the first year, you were allowed seven full hours of time every week for English, how many minutes in each week would you give to :—

	Speaking lessons	Reading lessons	Writing lessons	
			Copying	Dictation
First Term				
Second Term				
Third Term				

Argue about this with your friends.

For the practical teacher

1. Simple designs seen on drums, pots, and other articles will provide excellent practice for the very first lessons in penmanship.

2. In the early stages of penmanship when the pupils are practising the same letters many times, in a large size, the work may become uninteresting. As a little break, the teacher may have some fun with the letters by making pictures of them :—

79

Find the letters in these pictures :

This is a dog going through a door : only his tail can be seen.

This is S for Snake :

This is the head of an ox :

3. Upside down :

bq   hy   nu   fj   NZ

4. How many letters can you make ?

oaabogqp   lkhbdtf   gqyp

5. When the pupils begin to copy words, it is a good thing to arrange the work to be copied in sentence-patterns so that continuous practice is given in writing a fixed group :—

He has a book.	Where is my pen ?
He has a pen.	Where is my chair?
He has a chair.	Where is my book ?

80

6. Writing exhibitions are very useful to encourage pupils at all stages, especially if the pupils' parents are invited. The exhibitions should be arranged after talking with the teachers of the other classes, so that the Handwriting Exhibition will also show how the work in English progresses up the school.

CHAPTER IX

TRANSLATION

1. Translation (the use of the mother-tongue) cannot be completely shut out from the English lesson. Some teachers say, ' I forbid the use of the pupils' own language in my classes ; we use nothing but English in the English lessons.' That teacher has forgotten what goes on inside his pupils' heads. He cannot tell whether, or when, his pupils are thinking in their own language. For example, he may explain by means of lines and drawings, using English all the time, the words *long* and *short* ; as he speaks and draws lines on the blackboard his pupils say to themselves in their own language, ' Oh, yes ! Our word for that is . . . . . .' Translation is taking place, even though the pupil has said nothing aloud. That happens throughout the Course, and will continue to happen after the student has left school.

2. There are strong arguments against the use of translation as a method of teaching. Every language has its own set of habits : habits of word-order, habits of sentence- and phrase-patterns, habits of using certain words (especially structural words) not found in other languages.

It is impossible to get command of the habits of one language by using continually the quite different habits of another language. If a person has learned all his life to write with his right hand, it is very difficult for him to learn to write with his left hand ; he will certainly not do it by continually changing from right to left hand. He must put the pen in his left hand and keep it there, and go on practising.

Translation recalls the language habits of the mother-tongue, and is therefore an obstacle to the learning of the foreign language.

3. But there are also very strong arguments in favour of translation. The strongest one is that translation will occur anyway, no matter what the teacher tries to do. When struggling with a new English word, the pupil searches in his mind for the equivalent in his own language. When he finds it, he is happy and satisfied ; he has a pleasurable feeling of success.

But as soon as the English word has become perfectly familiar, there is no feeling of success in translating it, and the translation is dropped. The object of the teacher, therefore, will be to take the strangeness of the new word away as quickly as possible, and make the pupil quite familiar with it, so that there is no need for, and no feeling of usefulness in, the act of translation.

There are some words which cannot be understood without the help of translation, and in some cases it is not possible to find one word to translate one word and a fairly long explanation is necessary : *ago*, *quite*, *neat*, *to get up*, *once upon a time*.

Again, points in grammar often require the use of the mother-tongue, in order to explain them ; indeed, comparison with the home language on grammatical points is often very useful.

4. The essential point to remember is that the language will be learned quickly and correctly if two things are constantly aimed at :—

   i. the pupil must be trained to make the *direct* connection between the idea in the mind and the English word for it, whether the idea be an object (table, book, engine) or an action (walking, jumping, growing) or a relationship (to, from, by, with, quite, almost).

   ii. the pupil must be highly trained in English sentence- and phrase-patterns.

5. Translation is of no use for the second of these purposes ; it is, in fact, very unwise to use it except, very occasionally, to show the difference (or the likeness) between the English pattern and the vernacular pattern.

6. For the first purpose (vocabulary) translation should not be used when the direct connection can be made without it, by using objects, or pictures, or actions. Silent translation will go on at first, inside the pupil's head, but he will soon drop it if the ' direct method ' teaching is successful and interesting in itself. On certain occasions translation may be found very useful, and a great saver of time.

It is a safe guide for the teacher to use any method which will make things easy for the children, and which will give them a feeling of success and of being certain. The teacher will avoid at all times and by every means any possibility of giving his pupils a feeling of hopelessness, defeat and discouragement. These are golden rules, and apply to every branch of teaching English. Every time a pupil makes a mistake he feels downhearted because he has gone back a step ; therefore, let the work be done so thoroughly that when the pupil has to speak, or read, or write anything, he knows it so well that he gets it right the first time. If translation helps, use it ; if it is likely to lead to mistakes, avoid it.

7. These considerations may now be reduced to practical terms :—

    i. When teaching words, use English speech, objects, pictures, actions, and every possible means of making the direct connection between idea and word. Use translation *only after* all these methods have been used.

    ii. As soon as you fall back on translation, you are breaking the rules about giving the pupils plenty of listening practice, and about sentence-patterns. Therefore, if you do have to translate, get it over quickly and get back into English.

    iii. In higher classes, the use of the mother-tongue is valuable, sometimes necessary, in explaining points in grammar. Do not be afraid to use it for that purpose ; but again, as quickly as possible get back into English.

    iv. Translation can sometimes be used as a quick oral test of vocabulary in the form, ' What is the English word for . . . . . ? ' This should always be limited to single words and should *never* be used for sentences or phrases, because of the importance of practising the English, and not the vernacular, patterns.

    v. Free composition is really a very difficult form of translation (see paragraph 7 of Chapter VIII). It should never be attempted without most careful and thorough preparation, in order to

remove all the dangers—of making mistakes—
which the act of translating brings with it.

Points to think about and discuss

1. Remembering that open translation must be
avoided whenever possible (and objects, pictures,
actions used instead), but that sometimes the Direct
Method cannot be successful without unnecessary
waste of time, which of these words would you teach
by the Direct Method, and for which of them would
you fall back on translation ? For which would you
use both Direct Method *and* translation ?

a few	perhaps	neck	on
the second one	put	bone	wicked
rough	point to	alive	red
right (=correct)	grass	give	pick up

2. How are plurals formed in your language ? In
teaching English plurals to second-year pupils, would
you avoid translation, or would you use it ? How ?

3. Explain why it is true to say that free composition (like 'Describe a person you know') is
really an exercise in difficult translation unless it is
most carefully prepared for in lesson-time, before the
pupils begin to write.

For the practical teacher

1. Bearing in mind the rule that translation is
safest when it is confined to a single word, it is possible
to make one subject help another. For example, the
lessons in arithmetic can be made to help the lessons
in English.

When teaching numbers, the English numeral word
can be taught at the same time as the vernacular
numeral, and can be entered on the Number Wall

Chart if one is used :—

| 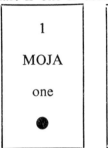 | 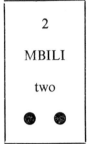 |  |

2. If a word is to be taught which cannot be explained by the Direct Method, but only by an explanation in the mother-tongue (for example, *ago*), never leave the pupil with only that one thin connection. Where translation is used in this way, it must be *at once* strengthened by repetition and practice, and always in patterns. Having explained the meaning of *ago* in the vernacular, drill the pupils at once in the *ago* pattern :—

Kazi was ill
{ two days ago.
three days ago.
a week ago.
a month ago.
a year ago.
some time ago.

3. If a pattern of the mother-tongue is very different from the English pattern for the same idea, the contrast should be made clear by translation drill.

What is the pattern in your own language for ' the best of all ' ? If it is very different from the English phrase, it can be drilled in this way :—

(*a*) Put on the blackboard :

This is | the best of all.

(b) Explain the difference between the pattern in the mother-tongue and the English pattern.

(c) Translate : This is / the longest of all. and one or two other examples.

(d) Give the adjective in English and let the pupils give the full sentence in English :—

Teacher :	shortest :	*Pupils* :	This is /the shortest of all
	quickest :		the quickest of all
	thickest :		the thickest of all
	thinnest :		the thinnest of all

(e) Give the vernacular sentence and ask the pupils to give you the English sentence.

4. Classroom orders, *in all lessons*, may be given in English, not in the mother-tongue. The children will translate at first, but very soon they will accept the English order without any trouble.

Clean the blackboard, please.
Answer your names, please.
Please give me the chalk.
Open the window, please.

CHAPTER X

GRAMMAR

1. Very few teachers find any pleasure in giving English grammar lessons, and very few pupils care for the subject either ; both teachers and pupils much prefer the reading lesson or even composition. To the teacher, grammar seems to be difficult to explain, uninteresting to teach, and the results appear to be unsatisfactory. To the pupil, grammar is often very confusing, hard to ' get right ', and it exposes his errors without seeming to be of much practical help.

The explanation lies in one simple fact : most teachers forget that grammar is not a separate subject like arithmetic or geography, but is only one small part of the English course. Having a separate class-book for it, and special lesson periods set apart as ' grammar lessons ', both teachers and pupils fail to see that grammar is not something to be studied alone but must go hand-in-hand with the reading lessons and the composition lessons ; on no account must it be treated as something apart from these.

The teacher and his class both dislike grammar because they try to do too much. If the grammar lessons are to be interesting (and therefore successful) the work done in them must be kept well behind, and never allowed to run in advance of the work which is being done in talking and reading.

2. In several places in this book we have found that very valuable guidance in teaching a foreign language can be obtained by thinking over what happens when a little child is learning his own language while he is still too young to go to school. It is clear

that a little child, picking up his own language from his mother and his family, never gets any special grammar lessons. Nevertheless, no matter how difficult his language may be, he learns to speak it accurately, and to use all the special word-endings for singular and plural, for tense, and all the other grammar 'rules'. How can he do this if nobody ever teaches him the ' rules ' of the grammar of his language ?

In the first place (as we learned in Chapter III), he is interested in objects and actions and not in separate words. He never hears a word spoken alone ; he always hears it in a sentence or in a phrase. When he is attracted by an object and is trying to learn its name, he hears that name used in various positions in various sentence-patterns. Sometimes he hears it in the singular number and sometimes (changed a little) in the plural number, so that it appears to him that the object he is interested in has at least two different names, similar to one another but not exactly the same. He gathers from the talk around him that one form of the name is used when only one object is meant, and the other form is spoken when two or three of the objects are talked about. This must puzzle the child, but he cannot fail to notice that the same thing happens with the names of all the other objects he wants ; and presently his young mind grasps the fact that the same changes occur, for the same reasons, in all the names he hears.

The next step he takes is to use that change in every noun he knows when he wishes to express (say) the plural and not the singular.

We know that this is true, because little children are heard to make grammar mistakes by using a common ' rule ' for words to which that rule does not in fact apply. Thus, a little English child will be heard to say, ' Two mans comed ' instead of ' Two men came,' because the child is using the plural *s* rule for *man* (to which the rule does not apply), and the past tense *ed* rule for *come* (again a special word which does not obey the ordinary rule for past tense). You will probably be able to think of similar mistakes which are made in your own language by little children.

3.   From this we can see what goes on in a child's mind when learning his own language and the grammar which belongs to it.   First, he is concerned *only* with as much of the language as he can already speak and use : that is to say, he pays attention only to changes in the names of the objects around him and of the actions which he can perform or understand. He pays no attention (because he cannot do so) to words which he does not need for his own speaking.

Secondly, his thoughts are not upon single words, but upon sentence-patterns ; and it is from these sentence-patterns that he picks out the changes which happen to a word according to its use in the pattern.

Thirdly, after he has noticed several times the same word-change, and has seen that all the words he knows of that kind undergo the same change, he thinks of all those words as a group to which one ' rule ' applies. He then uses that rule for all the words in the group and also for all new words he may learn of the same kind.

In most cases, this proves to be quite correct, but not always ; it sometimes leads him to make a mistake through applying his ' rule ' to a special word which does not really belong to the group.   These mistakes are corrected as he grows older and learns more of his language.   Thus, at first, an English child will use *spoon*, *spoons* ;   *cup*, *cups* ;   *man*, *mans* ;   later, he corrects this and says *man*, *men*.

What happens can be summarized like this :—

(a) the child deals only with the small vocabulary and the few sentence-patterns which he can use, and no more ;

(b) he forms groups of similar cases (like the *s* for plurals in English ;

(c) from these groups he makes for himself simple grammar ' rules'.

4.   This description of what happens in the case of a little child shows us why many teachers and classes find their grammar lessons difficult and uninteresting, and so dislike them.   They try to do too much.   In their lessons in grammar they try to cover more of the language than they have learned to use with ease in the talking and reading lessons.   They try to form and understand grammatical groups which include words and changes in meaning strange and new to them. They try to learn from the grammar book rules which are confusing because the book mentions also ' exceptions ' which the pupils have not yet met in their other English lessons.   In fact, they are trying to do grammar which is far in advance of their speaking and reading abilities.

5.   There is one more reason why grammar lessons are unpopular.   We have said that grammar is not a separate subject like arithmetic, but is only a small part of the whole work in English.   There is, in fact, no such thing as general ' grammar ' ; there are only various separate grammars, one for each language : such as English grammar, Russian grammar, Chinese grammar, and so on.   We have to teach, and our pupils must learn, not grammar in general but the particular grammar of English.   As we have seen in Chapter III, English grammar is not very difficult as it consists only of three things :—

(a) the ways in which English uses word-order to show meaning. These are learned through sentence-patterns and phrase-patterns ;

(b) the ways in which English uses structural words. These, too, are learned through examples in patterns ;

(c) the ways in which English uses a few inflexions, and the number of these is very small.

Grammar lessons are unpopular because too often many unnecessary difficulties are added to these three essentials of the English language.

6. We are now able to consider what we should include in the grammar work. First of all, when studying the kinds of words that make up the groups of examples upon which rules concerning word-order, structural words, and inflexions can be based, we must have names for them. These names are the Parts of Speech. Secondly, when studying how sentence-patterns are made, we must have names for the various parts of a sentence. These are grammatical names : Subject, Predicate, Qualifier, Object, etc. Thirdly, when studying changes in meaning, we must have special words to describe the kind of change we mean. These are such things as Tense (for changes in time), Active and Passive (for changes in the meaning of the verb), and Singular and Plural (for changes in the meaning of nouns).

English grammar must begin, therefore, with learning the meanings of these special grammatical words, and with practice in using them to describe the right things.

But this must all be done *within the limits of the vocabulary and sentence-patterns which are already thoroughly well-known to all the pupils.* Strange words and new examples must not be used. Grammar must follow, and not come before, ability to use (without reference to any grammar rules, but just through imitation, practice, and repetition) the language forms which are to be discussed.

It follows that the grammar book used in any class should contain just sufficient material to cover what the class has already done, or is doing, in the speaking and reading lessons. It should on no account deal with grammar problems connected with constructions, tenses, or meanings which the pupils have not yet learned to use in speaking. Grammar must go hand-in-hand with talking and reading ; these are carefully graded in the classbook ; the grammar book must be graded to agree with it.

7. When should grammar lessons begin to appear in the course ? The answer is clear : the pupils will only be puzzled and discouraged if grammar is intro-duced before they have had time to collect, in their speaking, a sufficient number of words and of sentence-patterns from which to select the ' groups ' that (in the grammar lesson) will receive their special gram-matical names, and from which the pupils will be able to build the first simple grammar rules.

Some schools may find that the easiest grammatical names (the Parts of Speech, and the main divisions of the sentence-pattern) can be safely begun in the third year of the course ; but it is extremely unlikely that this work can be undertaken earlier than that without puzzling the pupils and making the grammar lessons difficult, and therefore uninteresting. If grammar is postponed to the fourth year, all the better, for by then the pupils will have plenty of material to use and the grammar will appear to them to be ' easy ' ; the teacher will find few difficulties to explain and the whole class will have a feeling of success and progress.

The use of the special words needed in grammatical explanations, such as the names of the Parts of Speech, Number, Gender, Degree, Interrogative, Relative, Tense, and so on, will gradually become more frequent as the student goes through the English Course year by year.

8. If it is decided to begin to teach the easiest things (the names of the important Parts of Speech) in the Third Year, and to give the pupils by the end of the full Course the ability to name correctly and to describe the work done by the different parts of all the important sentence-patterns, the grammar work of the school may perhaps be arranged in three Steps each linked closely with the work in speech and reading :—

Step I :—

(1) The Parts of Speech, how they are formed, and to point them out in a sentence.

(2) The formation of the plural in the words so far learned.

(3) The use of the pronouns so far learned.

(4) The formation of phrases based upon prepositions, using the meanings in which the prepositions are used in the Reader.

(5) The uses of the structural verbs used in the Reader.

(6) The uses of the tenses as far as learned.

(7) The simplest inflexions.

(8) The construction of the phrase-groups used in the Reader of the year.

(9) The word-position of the nouns, verbs, adjectives, and adverbs met with in the Reader.

Step 2 :—

(1) The uses of new structural words, and new uses of old structural words, to express different

changes in meaning, and to form useful phrase-patterns.

(2) More inflexions.
(3) Verb changes.
(4) The description of further sentence-patterns and phrase-patterns met with in the Readers.
(5) Relatives and Clauses and the construction of sentence-patterns in which one part of the pattern is itself a sentence.
(6) Word-building : changing a word from one Part of Speech to another.

Step 3 :—General revision to cover :—

(1) The same word used as different parts of speech in different sentence-patterns.
(2) The work done by qualifiers of all kinds.
(3) The analysis of the chief sentence-patterns, including complex sentences.
(4) The analysis of the chief phrase-patterns.
(5) The uses of parts of the Verb.
(6) Adjectivals of all kinds.
(7) Adverbials of all kinds.
(8) Description in detail of the work performed in a sentence-pattern by any given word, or phrase, or clause.

9. A good modern grammar book will be built upon these principles and will be graded so as to fit in with the vocabulary and constructions which the pupil has learned at each stage.

The essential thing is to make quite certain :—

(i) that the grammar work is not more advanced than the reading work ;
(ii) that it is so graded as to appear easy and not difficult to the pupil.

When difficulty is removed, interest and pleasure in the work take its place.

Points to discuss

1. Make a list of the childish grammar mistakes which you have heard made by a young child learning your own language in its home. Explain each of the mistakes ; show how the child becomes cured of the error.

2. When did you first begin to learn English grammar ? Did you enjoy the lessons ? Were they successful in your case at that stage ?

If you found grammar difficult and uninteresting in your own schooldays, can you give reasons for it ? Were any of the principles discussed in the Chapter above disregarded ?

3. If you had to teach a British or an American person your own language, could you use English grammatical terms to explain it to him ? Are there any grammar rules in your own language which do not apply to English grammar ? What are they ?

4. Read again paragraphs 2 and 3 of this Chapter. At what point does the child begin to see the differences between the various Parts of Speech, although he does not know their grammatical names ?

5. Take this group of sentences (which will certainly be very well known to a pupil in his third year of English) and show how you would use them to point out the importance of word-order in English in these respects :—

    (i) in statements of this pattern ;
    (ii) in changing these statements into questions ;
    (iii) in the word-order of an adjective and its noun.
       This one is mine.   Kazi is working.
       The other man was in the house.
       Your brother is a policeman.

6. What sentence-pattern would you choose to help a class to find the rule for turning into a fixed question (i.e., a question which has for an answer a plain *Yes* or *No*) a statement in which the verb includes a structural verb ?

7. Make up three groups of nouns to show that the *s* or *es* of the plural in English is pronounced in three different ways :—

a hissing *s* ; a *z* sound ; and an *iz* sound.

8. In a class of pupils who have done five or six years of English, it will be necessary to show that one word may act as different parts of speech in different sentences.

Collect groups of sentences from which you could show that the same word may be :—

a noun in one sentence ; an adjective in another; a verb in another.

9. Look at the Exercises given in any good series of Readers and pick out, from the Reader for each year separately, Exercises which may be classed as :—
    (i) Exercises on sentence-patterns ;
    (ii) Exercises on phrase-patterns ;
    (iii) Exercises which are a preparation for grammar work ;
    (iv) Grammar exercises.

10. Write Notes for a Lesson in the Fourth Year of English on ' The formation of the comparative and superlative degrees in adjectives.' Use these headings:
    (*a*) The teacher's own list of adjectives which will be used in the lesson. (Preparatory oral work with objects and pictures).
    (*b*) The class is made to give a group of sentences in which the Comparative and Positive degrees of those adjectives are used.

97

(c) The class divides those groups into three :—
Positive degree sentences ; Comparative degree sentences ; Superlative degree sentences.

(d) The class is made to discover the rules.

(e) The class is taught the special names *Positive, Comparative, Superlative.*

(f) Oral exercises.

(g) Written exercises.

For the practical teacher

1. One very good way of teaching the parts of a sentence-pattern is to show the parts, not in words, but in a picture, whenever that is possible. For this purpose, a simple blackboard drawing is most useful :—

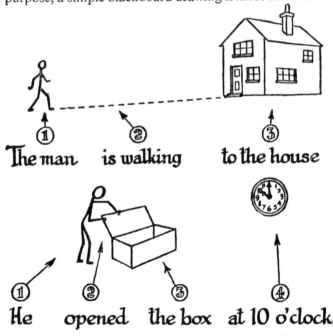

2. Another way of teaching the parts of a sentence-pattern is by means of questions. (This work, of course, is for more advanced students, not for the lower classes.)

Many teachers begin by making the pupils underline all the verbs, That is not easy to do ; it is uninteresting, and it leads very easily to mistakes.

Take, for example, this sentence which the class is to divide into its parts, phrases and clauses :—

When David was doing his written composition work yesterday he found in his exercise-book a scorpion which was half dead because it had lost two legs.

A student can easily make a mistake over the words *written* and *work* and mark them as verbs, which they are not. He will then find that he is badly wrong, will get discouraged, and will probably hate grammar.

But let it be done this way, through questions :—
What happened to David yesterday ?
(This gives the Main Clause and it is written down :
he found in his exercise-book a scorpion.)
When did he find it ?
(This gives the qualifier which tells us *when*, i.e., the adverbial clause. It is written down :—
When David was doing his written composition work yesterday.)
What was strange about the scorpion ?
(This gives the qualifier to the word *scorpion*. It is written down :— *which was half-dead.*)
Why was it half dead ?
(This gives the qualifier to the verb *was half dead.*
It is written down :— *because it had lost two legs.*)
These parts are now examined :—
(1) What is the most important statement ?
(That will be the Main Clause.)

    (2) What group tells us the time when ?
          (That will be the Adverbial Clause.)
    (3) What group describes the scorpion ?
          (That gives an Adjectival Clause.)
    (4) What group explains the reason why ?
          (That gives another Adverbial Clause.)

Try the same method with this sentence, where the object of the exercise is to pick out phrase-patterns :—

What questions would you ask the class in order to separate out the phrases from the Main Clause ?

Riding on our fast camels towards the Arab encampment we saw two old women with baskets of corn on their heads.

3. Grammar must be linked closely with the other work in English. For example, work on the Parts of Speech can be made a most useful help to vocabulary work, in this way :—

When teaching a Part of Speech (say a Noun), deal first with the form of the noun :—

    (*a*) most nouns are simple in form : box, cape, book.
    (*b*) others are marked by special endings : position, attention, direction.
    (*c*) others are made from action-words : builder, painter, writer, teacher.
    (*d*) others are made from describing-words : quickness, sadness, kindness.

A good grammar book (suitable for the teacher's own use) will suggest groups of this kind for all parts of speech.

4. Just as in Chapter IV it was suggested that the pupils should make lists of words under various classifications, so when they begin grammar there can be competitions to find out who can make the longest lists of nouns, adjectives, verbs, etc., from the words

they have learned to use.

5. Do all you can to see that grammar lessons are made interesting to the pupils. Here are some suggestions :—

(a) When teaching preposition phrases :—

Tell the class to imagine a scene well-known to them, say an important street near the school.

Tell them to shut their eyes and to ' see ' that street as if it were a picture or on the screen at the cinema.

Tell them to put people, animals, and things into the picture on the screen.

Then let them give, in turn, a description of the people and animals they can ' see on the screen.'

You will first give the pattern in each case :—

a man with a red coat; a woman with a baby;

a workman with a ladder ;

a boy with a mosquito on his neck.

a policeman in front of a shop ;

a soldier near a lamp-post ;

a dog behind a man ;

a bird on the roof of the cinema.

(b) When teaching Infinitive phrases :—

Let the pupils complete each of these in different ways :—

I know how to . . . . .
I know what to . . . . .
I know when to . . . . .
I know where to . . . . .

(c) When teaching -*ing* phrases :—

Let the pupils complete :—

I saw a man	singing in the rain.
I saw a man	-ing . . . . . .
I saw a boy	-ing . . . . . .
	etc.

6. When teaching structural words, for example, *do* :—

Let the pupils collect all the examples they can find of *do* between (say) Page 6 to Page 16 of their Reader. There will be much competition to see who can collect the largest number of examples.

The sentences which have been found can then be collected into suitable groups to teach the uses of *do*

(a) in questions : *Did he come ?*
(b) in negatives : *I don't like it.*
(c) to repeat a verb : *He writes better than I do.*
(d) for emphasis : *I do think he's unkind.*

7. Indirect Speech can be dramatized.
One student stands in front of the class and makes statements ; a second student then addresses the class and explains what was said. The class can then address the speaker, 'You said that . . . . .'

Speaker : I am opening this box.

Teacher : What did he say ?

Announcer : He said that he was opening that box.

Speaker : What did I say ?

Class : You said that you were opening that box.

102

8. At all times, quick blackboard sketches are most helpful in keeping the class amused and interested. The class supplies the words as the teacher alters the drawing :—

Adjectives :—

A man is walking to the house.

A man with a dog is walking to the house.

A man with a dog is walking to the house near the bridge.

Adverbs :—

      quickly   slowly   quietly

CHAPTER XI

SOME GENERAL SUGGESTIONS

In this Chapter, the writer of this book will tell you about his own experiences as a teacher of English as a foreign language to beginners in India and Burma.

1. *The need for change and variety*

There is no doubt that the pupils wish to learn English and that, when they begin, they come to the English lessons with more interest than they bring to any other lesson. They know that if they go home and show how their English is improving, their parents will be proud and pleased. This is most valuable to the teacher, but very often the eagerness dies away and is lost. It is killed by dull lessons and dull teaching ; and the fault is with the teacher, not with the pupil. The eagerness to learn, and the pleasure in making progress, will remain if the lessons are interesting so that the pupil can say, ' I like my English lessons.'

2. Lessons are dull and uninteresting when they are all the same. Change and variety among the lessons, and during each lesson, are necessary ; in fact, a lesson which is dull because it does not contain interesting changes of work is a very bad lesson—and the teacher is a bad teacher. A good teacher is one who keeps the pupils lively and interested, doing different things, all the time.

The very worst way to take a lesson is to open the reading-book, begin at the top of the page, and go working through it to the bottom of the page. There is no life or interest in such a lesson, but is it not very common ?

3. Different teachers will, of course, do different things in order to bring interesting changes of work into a lesson. Here is *one* of the ways I used, to keep my pupils interested and active in a lesson of forty minutes. Suppose the lesson was to teach some new words and a new sentence-pattern *There are . . . . .* The lesson begins :—

(a) 5 *minutes* : *Listening* : I picked up two or three objects whose names I wished to teach and began talking about them, as in *First Year English* : *What and How to Teach,* constantly bringing in the names of the objects and the phrase *There are . . . .* First I spoke to the whole class ; then I mentioned some names. ' Look, Kazi, this is a spoon, and this is another spoon. Can you see two spoons, Daud ? They are on the table. There are two spoons on the table, Luka. There are two spoons.'

Then I pretended somebody was coming in at the door. ' Oh, good-morning, Dr. Cook. I'm teaching my class about these two spoons. There they are, on the table.' And so on, carrying on an imaginary conversation with Dr. Cook.

Then suddenly I would turn to one of the pupils and start talking to him again. After that, I might go behind the blackboard, talking all the time, showing the spoons over the top of the blackboard, or round the side of it saying : ' Look ! There are two spoons under the blackboard. Now there are three spoons on the top of the blackboard. Where are they now ? Yes, there are four spoons here, at the side of the blackboard ' and so on.

In that way the first five minutes quickly passed, and the children were smiling at my tricks, but listening all the time.

(b) *Next 5 minutes* : *Imitation* : The class now had to imitate the words and imitate the phrase : ' There are two spoons on the table (on the chair) (on the floor) ' First they did it all together ; then separate pupils did it ; then each row of pupils ; then everybody whose name had the letter A in it (Daud, Luka, etc.). Then the class spoke the words with their eyes shut. Then they did it as they pointed to the place where the spoons were. Then they whispered the words. Finally, they sang them.

In that way the second five minutes passed and the children were still happy and interested.

(c) *Next 5 minutes* : *A break for a change* : In this 5 minutes we talked about some other sentence-pattern, using many different objects, but including the new objects of the lesson also, revising old work : ' This isn't a knife, is it ? ' The pupils knew the question forms which I used, so there were ' races ' to see who could answer first and quickest.

(d) *Next 5 minutes* : *Action* : *Teacher and Pupils* : In this 5 minutes, I called out one or two pupils, and we did a chain of actions together, moving the spoons (and other objects) about from the table, to the chair, then to the floor,

106

then under a book. (See para. 6, page 109.)

First we did it in silence—all the class watching to see what was going to happen next.

Then I did the actions, in exactly the same order, speaking, and the pupil copied me in silence. Then we both did the actions, both speaking. Then I would do the actions alone, but make a mistake in the order in which I did them, and the whole class would laugh and correct me.

(e) *Next 5 minutes* : Two or three pupils did the actions and spoke the words. Sometimes they would take special names, ' Dr. Cook ', ' Nurse Lili', and so on. Sometimes the class would say the words while the pupils did the actions without speaking. In that way, many pupils were practised until that 5 minutes passed.

(f) *Next 5 minutes* : *Work with the blackboard or with strips* : See Chapters V and VII of this book.

(g) *Next 5 minutes* : *Adding the new work to the old work* : First I did all the talking, using all the sentence-patterns which the pupils knew, employing old words as well as the new words.

(h) *Last 5 minutes* : Then I would ask the pupils if they could ' be the teacher ' and say all those sentences, handling the various objects. Finally, the class was drilled :—

There are two spoons on the table.
There are three books on the chair.
There are . . . ., *etc.*

This drill was done all together, separately, row by row, whispering, with eyes closed, standing, sitting, and in all sorts of other ways. Finally, we opened our reading books, and read, without any trouble at all, what we had been saying and doing all the lesson.

The 40 minutes had gone, and we had enjoyed ourselves.

4. *The need for activity*

Children are active little people, and their school must not be a sort of prison where they are forced to sit still. They must be allowed to be active ; to be doing things, and moving (at least moving their hands) nearly all the time.

The teacher should invent all kinds of actions for the pupils to perform with the objects, pictures and charts used in the English lesson. Let them be carried about ; let them be moved from one place to another ; let them be arranged in lines, in squares, in circles, in triangles, talking all the time.

5. I have had many happy lessons when teaching prepositions. Copying my actions, the pupils put (or held) their books or pencils in a given position and said the preposition. For example, putting the pencil on the desk, *on* ; under the desk, *under* ; near the floor, *near*. Then the same actions were performed, but this time the preposition was whispered. After that, there was a game of ' Where is it ? ' For this, a line of containers was placed on the top of a cupboard —a box, a bag, a tin, a pot, a cup. The class were then told to stand up, turn round with their backs to me, and close their eyes. I then quietly put something small into one of the containers.

The class then sat down in their seats facing me,
and the game began.

Where is it ? In the box ?   No.
                In the cup ?   No.
On the top of the cupboard ?   No.
                In the bag ?   Yes.
            It is in the bag.

What is it ?   Is it a pen ?   No.
               Is it a pencil ?   No.
        Is it a piece of paper ?   Yes.

            It is a piece of paper.

The piece of paper is in the bag.

6. Action chains are always very much enjoyed
by the pupils. The action chain is written on the
blackboard as orders :—

Come to the front of the class.
Walk round the blackboard backwards.
Touch the blackboard.
Go to the door.
Knock three times.
Go back to your place.

The chain is learned by heart, silently. (I always
helped the slower pupils by whispering to them.) Then

the blackboard is turned away from the class, and the action begins.

One pupil at a time can do it, saying, ' I'm coming to the front of the class. I'm walking round the blackboard backwards. I'm . . . ., *etc.*' Or three pupils can do it together, saying, ' We're coming, *etc.*' Or the pupils in front can act in silence and the rest of the class point and say, ' They're, *etc.*'

7. Then there is the action chain with an object :—
This is a box.
I have a box in my hand.
I'm opening the box.
I'm looking in the box.
There's a beetle in the box. (I really did pull out a beetle and show it to the class. Of course, I had put it there beforehand !)
This is the beetle.
I'm putting the beetle in the box.
I'm shutting the box.
I'm putting the box on the table.
I'm going to my place.

This action chain was repeated by many pupils until it was known by heart.

8. *Acting plays*

Such action-chains lead, by easy stages, to the acting of little plays. This is a most important form of work for providing activity by the pupils combined with speaking. Throughout this book it has been suggested that the teacher of English who will be most successful is the teacher who spends most of his time in getting his pupils to do things and to speak as they do them and who uses the class Reader for this purpose, instead of spending all the time in reading from the printed page.

The acting of little plays gives the pupils freedom from sitting still and answering a few questions ; it gives them opportunities for bodily movement joined with speaking ; and it makes the English work most interesting to them.

Every English class should be able to give once a term or once a year a little play, even if it lasts no more than fifteen minutes, and classes which are really good in English should give one lasting at least half an hour.

There are, however, three dangers which the teacher must avoid. First, the class should not be asked to do too much, in language which is too difficult for them. If that happens, far too much time will be spent in practising the words and actions and only a few of the very best pupils in the class will be able to take part, while the remainder lose interest.

Secondly, the teacher may be tempted to use a little play (performed by the best pupils) as a sort of show, pretending that the class pupils are better in English than is really the case. Acting a play is one of the ordinary direct methods of teaching English ; it is not an advertisement. The object is to help all the pupils with their English through an interesting exercise, not to please visitors to the school.

Thirdly, there is the danger of choosing subjects which appear to be in easy English but are not suitable to the age of the pupils in the class. It is very bad teaching to make a big strong boy, or a tall girl, say in public completely unsuitable nursery rhymes which in England are meant only for tiny children. The pupils find out the truth sooner or later and then they feel that they have been made to look foolish.

9. The first step towards the use of plays as a method of teaching English is the expansion of one of

the speech-and-action exercises by the introduction of other speakers. For example, taking the action-chain given in paragraph 7 on page 110, the expansion could be as follows.

A : This is a box.
    B : I beg your pardon ?

A : This is a box. I have a box in my hand.
    B : Yes, I can see it. (to C :) Can you see the box ?
    C : Yes, there it is. I can see it in his hand. (to A) What are you doing with it ?

A : I'm opening the box.
    C (to B) : Look, B ! He's opening the box.
    B (to A) : Is there anything in it ?

A : I'm looking in the box. There's a beetle in the box.
    B and C together : What !

A : There's a beetle in the box.
    B : Where is it ?
    C : Show it to us, please.

A : This is the beetle.
    B (to C) : Is it dead ?
    C (to B) : I don't think so. C (to A) : Please put it back.

A : I'm putting the beetle in the box.
    C (to B) : I don't like beetles. Tell him to shut the box.
    B (to A) : We don't like beetles. Please shut the box.

A : I'm shutting the box. I'm putting the box on the table.
    B and C (together, to A) : Thank you very much.
    B : Is that finished ?

A : Yes. I'm going back to my place.

B (to C) :   *We must go back to our places, too.*

10.   In elementary English courses there are usually some stories written in the form of little plays.   One or two of these should be chosen for special practice and presentation before an audience.

When it is decided that the class will try to act a little play, it is important that *all* the class should take part ;   the work must not be limited to a few pupils. This can be arranged in the following ways :—

(a) Each speaking part should be given to two or three, or more pupils, so that the play can be performed two or three times with different actors.   There will then be much competition between the teams of actors to see which team can perform the play best.   Senior pupils from the top class in the school, or other teachers, can be asked to be ' captains ' of the teams and give them extra training out of school hours.   Lists of the names of pupils, with the names of the characters they have to take in the play, should be put up on the Class Notice Board.

(b) A Committee should be elected from the pupils in the class to arrange for and provide the articles required for the play.   These need not be very difficult to obtain :   the teacher's desk can in one scene be disguised as a shop ;   in another as an office ;   in another, a hill ;   a basket can be just a basket in one scene, and a treasure of diamonds in another, and so on.

(c) The play should be carefully examined to find out what part the class as a whole can play. For example, in one scene, the class can be a crowd of people ;   in another, it can make the

113

noise of thunder ; in another, it can roar to represent a lion ; and so on, as required. Generally, the class can be used to make ' noises off the stage'.

(d) It is the duty of each actor to learn his speeches by heart. In lesson time, the pupils can test one another (in very soft voices), one pupil holding the book and the other saying his part of the play from memory.

A good teacher will find no difficulty in making the acting of a little play an extremely valuable part of the English work for the year.

13. *Things to use*

You will require many different objects, of many different kinds, to use in the English lessons : small stones, large stones, small boxes, tins, cups, small pots, two old knives, two balls of string, one or two balls (soft and hard), short sticks and long sticks, pieces of paper of different shapes, sizes and colours (at least two of each), some bottles of different colours and sizes, pieces of cloth, some leaves, books of different sizes and colours, long pencils, short pencils, pens, nibs, pieces of chalk, a small mirror, and many other articles. In addition, pictures of all kinds. (see Chapter I : *For the practical teacher*.) The teacher should not collect all these himself. The pupils will be pleased if they are asked to help.

14. The objects should be frequently changed. It is very dull if the same old objects are produced every lesson. ' Bring something for tomorrow's lesson ' is a good order to give ; it does not matter much what the children bring ; everything can be used at least once, and the most useful articles can be added to your collection, the others being quietly put away

without discouraging the pupils who brought them.

15. It is a mistake for the teacher to make all the flash-cards, wall charts, etc., himself. The pupils will be pleased to be allowed to help. ' Ask your father to make one like this ; we will do the writing in school ' is a good order to give sometimes. The parents will be pleased if the teacher visits them sometimes in order to get their help in making things for the English classes.

16. If possible, wall charts should not be rolled up ; they get torn, and they will not lie flat on the wall or on the blackboard. Big ones can be kept hanging flat on the back of a cupboard. Or they may be put in charge of a pupil who carefully brings them to school when wanted.

17. Material hung up on the wall must not remain there more than fourteen days. Children dislike having the same thing in front of them all the time, day after day.

18. Slot-charts (see Chapter IV) can be in two sizes ; large ones for the teacher and small ones for each pupil. The children should make their own, getting help from their parents where necessary. They will like to be allowed to do that.

19. You can have much fun, and do a lot of good work, with jointed dolls made of wood or cardboard ; the children will be happy to get their fathers to make them and paint them.

Use them for sentences like :—
He is walking. She is dancing.
They are dancing.

Or in the past tense :—
He walked across the table. Then he sat on the teacher's book.

115

20. Three or four match-boxes glued together make a ' street of houses ' or a ' train', in which to keep letters, or words, or divisions of a sentence-pattern :—

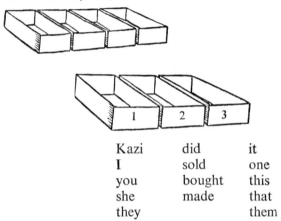

Nouns   Verbs   Preps.   Adjs.

1   2   3

Kazi	did	it
I	sold	one
you	bought	this
she	made	that
they		them

All the Subjects would be kept in Box No. 1 ; all the Verbs in Box No. 2 ; and all the Objects in Box Bo. 3.

21. The great thing to remember is to allow the *children* to bring, make, or help to make, or ask their parents to make, whatever you want. The English words can be added in school.

22. *Correction by the teacher*

Always be very kind and gentle when correcting a mistake : on no account must a pupil be allowed to get discouraged. Best of all, have no mistakes, by arranging that the work is so well done orally that the pupils will not make any errors in writing. If there are many mistakes, that is a sign of bad teaching : mistakes are not a sign that the pupils are lazy or bad.

Too many mistakes mean that the pupils are unhappy and discouraged, and that is the fault of the teacher. It is generally due to too much work in the Reader and not enough speech-work.

I once heard a teacher correcting a mistake like this :—

Pupil : He go to the door.

Teacher : He go ? Oh no ! Not *he go*. That is quite wrong. You mustn't say *he go*. Class, why is *he go* wrong ?

That was bad teaching. The teacher, by repeating the mistake was actually teaching it by listening, by speech, and by imitation. *Never repeat a mistake* : drill the correct form.

23. 'Marking' is necessary sometimes, but the pupils do not like it, and they do not pay much attention to it. The only way to deal with mistakes is to prevent them, by very thorough preparation of everything which is to be written. We do not *want* our pupils to make mistakes ; we do not want to lay traps for them to fall into. By setting work which is too difficult, or which has not been carefully prepared through speech, we set traps and almost compel our pupils to make mistakes. Then we put red marks on their books and blame them. That is not fair.

24. *Drawing*

Teach yourself to draw. It is quite easy and it will make a very great difference to the enjoyment of your lessons.

First, match-stick drawings of people :

The body is 2½ times the length of the head.

The legs are 1½ times the length of the body.

The arms are not quite long enough to reach the knees.

You can make the figures look to the left, to the right, up or down, just by putting a little mark for the nose :—

The hands are shown by a little curly mark :—

Watch children in various positions in order to get the arms and legs right :—

25. A box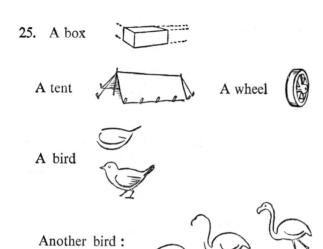

A tent

A wheel

A bird

Another bird :

26. A line of boxes, or ' houses ' or a ' train ' :

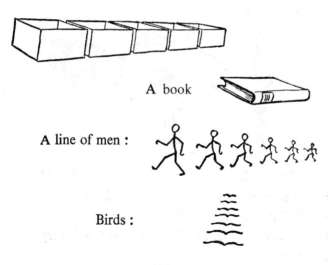

A book

A line of men :

Birds :

119

27. High up :

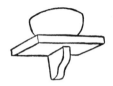

Level with the eye :

Below the eye :

28. Trees :

I found that quick drawing on the blackboard added a lot of fun to the lessons and the pupils were greatly interested. Speak in English all the time you are drawing, and let the children draw too, if they wish to do so.

29. *Meeting other teachers*

Staff meetings are very useful indeed, but before each one a list of things to be talked about should be collected from the teachers by the headmaster :—

Difficulties which the teachers of upper classes want the teachers of beginners to deal with.

Things seen in other schools.

New ideas for apparatus.

School exhibitions of pupils' work.

Helping one another to get, or make, things for use in class.

Common mistakes, and how to cure them.

Visits to one another's classes.

Keep a notebook of subjects to be discussed at your Staff meetings.

30. Visits to neighbouring schools are very important and extremely useful. It is well worth the trouble of arranging that each teacher should have one day off every term in which to visit a neighbouring school. You will see there new kinds of charts, new kinds of pictures, and you will get new ideas. You should invite teachers from other schools to come and see you at work, and compare notes.

31. Teachers' Associations for the purpose of arranging lectures on the teaching of English are very valuable.

The best form of lecture, and one that all teachers like to attend, is the lecture in which the speaker has a small class of young pupils on the platform with him.

I gave courses of lectures of that kind every year, and teachers used to come long distances by train to attend them. For the first twenty or thirty minutes I explained the principles of teaching which I was going to demonstrate with the class—it might be one of the paragraphs in this book.

I then called my little class of pupils (ten pupils are sufficient) to the desks on the platform which were placed there for them. I had all the necessary objects ready, and blackboard and chalk. Then I gave a lesson, with all the changes, like those described in paragraph 3 of this Chapter.

Sometimes (to show that I had not prepared the class specially for the lecture) I asked the teachers present to suggest something for me to teach. In that way the lecture was a kind of entertainment, as well as a piece of serious work.

Any teacher can do that—you have only to give the kind of lesson you like best, and all the teachers who come to hear you will enjoy it.

32. Children differ widely, and so do teachers. The best that any writer of a book like this can do is to suggest things for teachers to think about. Think about the suggestions made in this book ; alter them ; add to them ; and try to make each year of your teaching more interesting for the pupils and more thorough, in everything you do, than the year before.